# ECONOMY AND COMMUNITY

## Economic and Social History of Pre-Industrial England, 1500–1700

ROSEMARY O'DAY



Adam & Charles Black
London

FIRST PUBLISHED 1975
A. & C. BLACK LTD
4, 5 & 6 SOHO SQUARE, LONDON W1V 6AD

ISBN 0 7136 1573 7

PRINTED IN GREAT BRITAIN BY
HAZELL WATSON AND VINEY LTD
AYLESBURY, BUCKS

# Contents

# Introduction

This series, of which Dr Rosemary O'Day's book forms a part, is intended for students working in the sixth form or at undergraduate level. The authors were asked to assume that their readers had a basic foundation in the sixteenth and seventeenth centuries. The manner of approach is intended to be thought-provoking, and to invite discussion. The extracts which accompany the arguments may be read both in relation to the text and in their own right. Numbers in square brackets are used to identify the extracts which are all placed at the back of the book.

G. M. D. Howat

To my parents

# Preface

This short book does not present a chronological survey of the economic and social history of early modern Britain but attempts to study in some detail seven interrelated topics within that framework. Much original research, both completed and in progress, is inaccessible to both sixth formers and their teachers. While it may be accessible to the undergraduate or college student, it often seems extremely specialist in approach and completely divorced from the major historical issues of the period. What I have tried to do in the following studies is to provide a synthesis which introduces the student to new material and demonstrates clearly the significance of these original, detailed researches to wider themes. In such a short work it has obviously not been possible to include mention of all recent research on related matters, nor to do justice to much of that which is discussed. I hope, however, to have said enough to stimulate thought, discussion, and further reading.

I should like to acknowledge my debt to Dr B. A. Holderness who read the manuscript in full and to my husband, Dr Alan O'Day, who has offered constructive criticism at all times and read and re-read the work in manuscript. Mrs Joyce Powell deserves special mention for typing the manuscript both quickly and accurately. I am grateful to the staff of the Public Record Office, the British Museum, the Bodleian Library, Lichfield Joint Record Office, the Staffordshire County Record Office, the Lambeth Palace Library, Norfolk and Norwich Record Office, and the Leicester Record Office for permission to quote manuscript material. I have acknowledged my debt to the authors of works mentioned in the text in the select bibliography, but would like to thank Dr L. A. Clarkson individually for permission to reproduce the table on page 15. Finally, I thank the general editor of this series, Mr G. M. D. Howat, for his helpfulness and guidance.

Rosemary O'Day
University of Birmingham

# 1

# Population and the Price Rise

Currently there is a strong awareness of the impact of population movements, both up and down, upon the human condition in its economic, physical, cultural and environmental aspects. Historians also are showing interest in demographic change, not only for its own sake but for its demonstrable effects in other areas. Unlike the modern demographer, however, the historical demographer encounters great difficulties, occasionally insuperable, in amassing adequate data regarding the size of population in any country at any given point in time before the mid-nineteenth century.

How do historians set about establishing crude population figures for the England of 1500 to 1700 when there are no national censuses before that of 1801? The major records at the English historical demographer's disposal are censuses, taxation returns, and surveys for military purposes. Each of these types of source is open to criticism and all are few in number for the period concerned.

The most significant population counts of the sixteenth and seventeenth centuries undoubtedly take the form of ecclesiastical censuses. In 1547 the parsons and churchwardens of parishes were required to make returns of all the *housling* people in their parishes, and these documents are known as the Chantry Certificates. Unfortunately, the census was not of all people in the parish but of houslings, which probably means communicants. At this time the age at which Communion was compulsory was probably still 13 or 14. In order to establish the size of the whole population, historians have to arrive at an estimate of the omitted population of children and adolescents. They base this approximation upon the evidence of adult population and upon what they know of contemporary birth and mortality rates among the young. In 1563 the Privy Council ordered another ecclesiastical census [1], which listed the number of households in each parish. In order to arrive at the entire population a prudent multiplier, being an estimate of the average size of household, has to be employed. Thus, if the average size of household is accepted as five, and the number of houses in a parish is given as 35, the *approximate* population would be 35 times 5, equalling 175 persons. The accuracy of such estimates rests entirely with the correctness of the multiplier and with the accuracy of the original count of households. The count of 1563 was followed in 1603 by another ecclesiastical survey which listed numbers of communicants. By this time the accepted age of compulsory Communion was 16 and account has to be taken of this in supplying the missing portion of the population. A fourth religious count—the Compton census—which asked for the same information as that of 1603, was undertaken in 1676. It is to an extent suspect because the numbers of Nonconformists appear to have been underestimated. Lists of communicants were published by Dalrymple in 1688 and 1696 but there is reason to believe that figures for the ecclesiastical province of York were merely an estimate based upon the figures gathered for the province of Canterbury. Along with these large ecclesiastical censuses may be considered the Protestation Return of 1641–2, which was not ecclesiastical in origin but in effect provided a listing of all males in the villages of England and Wales over 18 years of age. As a result, the age- and sex-structure of the England of that time becomes a matter of paramount importance to the historical demographer if he is to supply the missing population.

In dealing with any count drawn up for the purposes of taxation—the second major source of population material—the historian must remember that the pecuniary purpose far outweighed the census motivation. Paupers and children are often disregarded in the returns and, as the proportion of the poor and the age beneath which children were regarded as untaxable remain exceedingly difficult to gauge, these omissions can prove an insuperable obstacle to accurate estimates. The most common taxation unit was not, however, the adult or even the adult male but the family or household, for reasons of administrative convenience. The Hearth Tax returns of 1662–74 are a major source of information concerning the population of England during this period. Preliminary returns for the Marriage Duty of 1695, which was a tax on bachelors and childless widowers as well as on married men, also provided useful population data, which was utilised by Gregory King, the late-seventeenth-century political arithmetician. King was able to use the Hearth Tax return of 1690 also to arrive at a population estimate from its information on number and size of households. Clearly, the successful use of tax-return material depends very much upon knowledge of the size of households within a given environment.

The third major source of material concerning the overall size of population is the muster roll. These are lists of all males liable for military service, in what Dr Christopher Hill has described as 'the home guard of property', who appeared at local musters at various dates. They are valuable chiefly in that they survive in reasonably large numbers, often with good chronological coverage of individual counties, and have been used to show relative differences in population size between county and county over a period of time. Repetition of names on a large scale, possibilities of evasion, problems of emigration and immigration, and the fact that they omit not only children, adolescents, women, elderly men and the disabled but also 'the meaner sort of people and servants', have made historians somewhat wary of their usefulness, however, and they certainly seem of doubtful value in demonstrating local population increase and decline or the actual size of the whole population.

Already some of the objections to the sources available have been listed—the difficulty of supplying the missing sections of the community; the imprecise nature of many of the listings; the difficulty of arriving at a generally acceptable multiplier. Added to these should be the fact that those who compiled early modern censuses demonstrated an inordinate love of round numbers when enumerating people, houses or hearths. As a result, many of the figures which they provided are in themselves approximations. This means that the historian, when calculating total population using either a multiplier or a corrective for missing sections of the population, is running a double risk of gross error. Historians also have reason to object that nation-wide or province-wide surveys, while receiving their inspiration from the top, nevertheless may have been compiled according to the varying criteria of the local collectors rather than the fixed ones of the central organisation.

Where several censuses exist over a reasonable period for a given county or area, it is possible for historical demographers to test the feasibility of the returns according to current knowledge of probable birth and death rates. For example, it seems highly unlikely in the light of such knowledge that a population could increase by more than three per cent per annum, except by the agency of large-scale immigration, and even then not for a long period. Historians, therefore, can compare population counts to obtain the rate of growth according to their results—if the rate of growth as shown between the different counts is fantastic, then it becomes clear that one or both of the censuses is highly inaccurate. Historians do, of course, analyse the data internally for further defects.

Historians of England and Wales and of western Europe in general have concluded that there was a general growth in population between 1500 and 1750—normally accepted as the first sustained increase since that of the thirteenth century. Historians are less able to agree upon the exact extent of this rise and upon fluctuations which occurred during this

250-year period. That this is so was inevitable in view of the scattered geographical coverage of the available resources and the aforementioned defects of their format. The table opposite gives a general idea of the magnitude of the increase in population. However crude the statistics, the general trend is sufficiently marked that the historian may assume that this rise in population must have had deep-reaching effects in society. It is part of the economic historian's task to discover just what these consequences were: to examine economic trends in the spheres of prices, wages, agriculture, urbanisation, internal and international trade, changes in living patterns, and so forth, and to decide to what extent population growth or decline contributed to them. In many cases it is a matter of deciding upon the degree of responsibility to be apportioned to demographic change rather than a question of attributing any importance at all to such change.

*The Price Revolution: its character and causes*

Historians agree that the sixteenth century witnessed a European price rise. Several attempts have been made to chart the rise in English basic foodstuffs and the most satisfactory of these is the Phelps–Brown price index of 1956 which covers the period 1264–1954. The index is based upon the cost of the shopping basket of goods purchased by a southern English family: adjustments were made for changes in dietary patterns —such as the substitution of the potato for peas during the nineteenth century—and the basket's mix contained a higher proportion of basic foodstuffs than industrial goods. According to the index, prices of such consumables tripled over the period 1500–80 and quadrupled by 1600. But such a bald statement as this conceals the fact that there were marked peaks and troughs in the movement of prices before 1580, with periods of relative stability between 1474 and 1509 and 1558 and 1570, a sharp drop in the late 1550s, and an accelerated rise in the late 1540s and early 1550s. Now in comparison with the rates of inflation in twentieth-century Britain, a quadrupling of prices over a hundred-year period seems scarcely to warrant the title 'revolution' but it should be remembered that this price rise followed a period of great stability in prices and that, moreover, the sixteenth-century economy was less adaptable and able to cope with the situation than its twentieth-century counterpart. Also, rising food prices affected adversely the living standards of a greater proportion of the population than ever before, because more people were dependent entirely upon wage earnings and were forced to purchase their consumables.

Historians have proffered many different explanations of the price

TABLE I ESTIMATES OF POPULATION, 1480–1750[1]

| Year | England | England and Wales | Source |
|---|---|---|---|
| 1480s | 2.1m | – | Cornwall |
| 1500 | – | 2.5 – 3.0m | Tucker |
| 1522–5 | 2.3m | – | Cornwall |
| 1545 | 2.8m | – | Cornwall |
| 1545 | – | 3.5m | Tucker, after Russell |
| 1570 | 2.8m | 3.5m | See text |
| 1603 | 3.75m | – | Cornwall |
| 1603 | – | 4.1m | Tucker, after Russell |
| 1650 | – | 5.5m | Wrigley |
| 1695 | – | 5.2 – 5.5m | Glass, after Gregory King |
| 1700 | – | 5.8m | Griffith |
| 1710 | – | 6.01m | Griffith |
| 1720 | – | 6.05m | Griffith |
| 1730 | – | 6.01m | Griffith |
| 1740 | – | 6.01m | Griffith |
| 1750 | – | 6.25m | Griffith |

References

Julian Cornwall: 'English Population in the Early Sixteenth Century', *Ec.H.R.*, 2nd ser., vol. xxiii, April 1970, pp. 32–44.

G. S. L. Tucker: 'English Pre-Industrial Population Trends', *Ec.H.R.*, 2nd ser., vol. xvi, Dec. 1963, pp. 205–8.

J. C. Russell: *British Medieval Population*, 1948.

E. A. Wrigley: 'A Simple Model of London's Importance in Changing English Society and Economy, 1650–1750', *P&P*, no. 37, 1967, pp. 48–9, 56.

D. V. Glass: 'Gregory King's Estimate of the Population of England and Wales, 1695', *Population Studies*, vol. iii, 1948–9, p. 358.

G. T. Griffith: *Population Problems in the Age of Malthus*, 1926.

[1] Taken from L. A. Clarkson, *The Pre-Industrial Economy in England*, Batsford 1971.

rise. These may be divided into several groups—monetary explanations, physical or real explanations, and multi-causal explanations. Until the 1950s the monetary theories were generally accepted as the most convincing. Earl J. Hamilton, working on the imports of American silver into Seville, produced some figures which showed an apparently close correlation between the extent of these imports and the rise in Spanish prices. During the 1950s other historians began to challenge this interpretation. With regard to England the theory that an increase in the quantity of money in circulation, via importation of silver bullion, was wholly responsible for the upward price movement seemed doubtful. Firstly, the price rise in Britain began some thirty years before imports of American silver to Seville reached a significant level in 1545 with the opening of the great Peru silver mine of Potosi, and, in fact, English prices had already doubled since the beginning of the century. Moreover, there is no evidence of continuous large-scale bullion imports into England even after 1545. An extremely favourable trade balance might have effected a significant inflow of specie, but it is normally accepted that this situation did not prevail during the sixteenth century. Certainly the relatively few captures of Spanish treasure ships by Englishmen can have had little effect upon the total amount of bullion in circulation. Perhaps most detrimental of all to Hamilton's case is the fact that the quantity-of-money theory in no way explains why food prices rose so much more rapidly than other prices.

This fact alone seems to point towards an explanation of the English price revolution in terms of supply and demand. This may be simply expressed: the population of England and Wales was rising faster than the available food supply. The Phelps-Brown index demonstrates that the price of basic foodstuffs such as barley (far more common than wheat in the sixteenth-century diet) were very hard hit by the price rise. The suggestion is that demand was overtaking supply. Historians, as has been shown, vary in their estimates of the rate of population growth and the actual size of population. Some believe that population grew by 40 per cent between 1500 and 1600 and actually doubled by 1660. Estimated size of population in 1500 ranges from 2.5 million to 3 million for England and Wales, with a general feeling that the higher is the more likely figure. Historians are less agreed in their approximations of population size for the end of the century—figures of 4 or 5 million being suggested. Whatever the figure accepted, a rise of something like 33⅓ per cent is posited over the century. Such a rise was significant and the thesis is attractive on these grounds alone, but the historian seeking an explanation of the price rise in real terms has to solve two problems: was the rate of agricultural production unable to accommodate this rate of population growth? Can the undoubted fluctuations in the rate of the price rise be correlated with fluctuations in demographic pressure?

The first of these questions can be asked in several ways. Was there sufficient agricultural surplus of the right kind in 1500 to cater for a natural increase in population of one-third without significant modification? If not, were the methods employed to solve the deficiency adequate and what expansion did they produce? To the first question the answer is no. Despite the fact that historians have overemphasised the self-sufficiency of individual medieval communities to the detriment of our knowledge of farming for the market, it is nevertheless clear that a community tended to put under plough only sufficient land to supply its own needs and the market needs of its hinterland. There was, of course, a certain amount of exporting of food, but grain export never formed more than a small proportion of English export trade and certainly in the sixteenth century a contraction in the amount of grain exported would have done little to remedy deficiencies in the supply of grain for the market at home. Assuming then that there was a real need for expansion in agricultural production, particularly in view of the fact that a higher proportion of the population than ever before was living in towns and agriculturally unproductive, what was done?

There is certainly evidence of changes in land use and techniques during the sixteenth and early seventeenth centuries. Regional specialisations, although not as exclusive as sometimes implied, were growing. For example, the potential of the Midland region for pastoral farming was appreciated and a land previously given over mainly to tillage was gradually transformed into one devoted to grazing animals. In other areas the transformation was less dramatic—the barren soils of the Peak District, the Lake District, the moorlands of the north-east, the Welsh mountains and the western moors were totally unsuited to profitable arable farming and continued to be devoted to sheep rearing; the Home Counties concentrated to an ever-increasing decree upon mixed husbandry and grain production, a traditional tendency intensified by the new demands of the London market. New techniques were also in use. In lowland England the needs of the population, and of the urban wage-earning population in particular, and the needs of the cloth industry, stimulated by home demand but more by the state of the export market, inspired a search for fresh grazing lands for stock. One answer lay in the conversion of land to convertible husbandry [3]. A field would be tilled for 2 to 12 years and then put under grass for a period of 7 to 12 years; a rotation between fields was practised. This system did not substantially depress the output of arable crops but did provide more land for grazing than traditional methods. Moreover, the grass produced was of high quality and the manured land for tillage was highly fertile. The method maintained the quantity and heightened the quality of both crops and livestock. This system was adopted in areas such as the Vale of Evesham where land had never before been ploughed. It replaced the shifting husbandry of much of lowland Northumberland and Durham; it took a strong hold in the Midlands, where between 1560 and 1660 about half the land came under 'up and down' husbandry. The introduction of the system was made easier in areas of enclosed land and was accompanied by enclosing and engrossing in other regions [2].

In other areas of England fens were drained and marshes and saltings reclaimed. Unfortunately the projects were often of limited success, sometimes for lack of technical expertise but more frequently because of natural disadvantages. The new lands were subject to wind erosion; their initial fertility was short-lived because they were now deprived of the necessary alluvial deposits, and yields were therefore low.

In the vales of Shropshire, Herefordshire and Somerset in the late sixteenth century the opposite technique was employed with some success—the floating of the water meadows. Under this system the meadows were irrigated in the late autumn. Flood waters deposited silt and protected the land from frost until late March when the land was drained. Then the sheep were let on to the land to graze. Eventually the land was re-flooded in preparation for the hay crop and after this turned over to cattle grazing in the late summer.

To a certain extent the sixteenth century saw the introduction of new crops, although this was more characteristic of seventeenth-century husbandry when turnips and carrots were introduced to Suffolk and legumes and improved grasses such as clover found their niches in areas of convertible husbandry and the lighter soils.

However, there is a danger that the historian will see such new methods as typical of sixteenth- and seventeenth-century agriculture as a whole whereas, in fact, they were typical rather of the extensive farms of those landowners who had sufficient capital to introduce them. Fen drainage was a major project which one great landowner, even, would find a strain to finance individually. The floating of water meadows, the introduction of convertible husbandry, and the enclosing and engrossing of land on a large scale all involved expenditure beyond the means of any but the large landowners. It is true, however, that the price revolution in foodstuffs of which we are talking had a boosting effect upon the farmers' incomes and gave many the necessary capital to make improvements.

Important though the changes in land use, farming techniques and organisation were, the historian is tempted to conclude that 'all that sixteenth-century agriculture seems to have achieved was the avoidance of a spiral of soil exhaustion and falling yields which could have led to a catastrophic decline in lower class living standards, comparable with the late thirteenth century'. (S. Pollard and D. Crossley: *The Wealth of Britain*, p. 95.)

The student of agricultural improvements in pre-industrial society would do well, however, to heed the warning of Professor Ralph Davis who has pointed out that if farmers benefiting from the pressure of population upon available foodstuffs had the resources to improve their techniques in raising grain and other consumables they did not have the incentive. 'It was not, as modern analogies have led some historians to suppose, the pressure of demand for corn in the period of rising population that led to the improvement of corn yields in western Europe. The reverse was the case: Netherlands agriculture was reorganised in the fifteenth century in response to falling, not rising, prices; the first country to follow whole-heartedly was England under the influence of declining corn prices after 1650; and in France advance came during the low prices of the second quarter of the eighteenth century. It was the easing of the relentless pressure to a corn monoculture that, paradoxically, disseminated the discovery that mixed farming would dramatically increase arable yields while maintaining or improving the farmer's profits during periods of low corn prices.' (Ralph Davis: *The Rise of the Atlantic Economies*, p. 117.)

The consequences of this failure to expand dramatically agricultural production are various: chief amongst them seem to be two, that there was heavy pressure upon available food supplies, resulting in high prices and also moves towards internal colonisation; that the population—or rather the poorer sections of that population—tended to be undernourished. It is a commonplace of textbook economic history that the wages of agricultural workers remained low, especially in comparison with rising prices, because of the abundance of labour. It was certainly true that there was no increase in the demand for food proportionate to the increase in population but, as food demand tends to become inelastic—because food is an essential of life—and as there was an urban population, rising faster than the rural population, which had to buy its food, the level of demand was greatly increased over the 150 years from 1500 to 1650. Because prices were high, particularly for basic foodstuffs, it is easily appreciable that the emphasis of the poor man's diet would be increasingly upon the traditional staple product—cereal crops—and that, as a result, the rise in cereal crop prices would be even more dramatic than that of other commodities. The argument involving levels of nutrition is important in demonstrating the interaction between demographic, economic and environmental factors. Because the poorer sections of the community were undernourished, owing to a combination of the high price and the scarcity of food, they were unable to resist the effects of natural disasters such as the plagues endemic in sixteenth-century Europe. This fact may be demonstrated with reference to the influenza epidemic of 1558 which resulted in high mortality and occurred after a series of poor and bad harvests. (It should be stressed here that these arguments do not apply to the period after circa 1650 when it is difficult to detect a direct correlation between harvest failure and increased mortality due, partially, to improved agricultural productivity and a falling-off in population increase which, in turn, improved the lot of a substantial sector of the farming community.)

In a total way, then, the effects of demand and supply upon the level of prices may be demonstrated, but it remains for the historian to correlate changes in the demographic pattern with changes in the movement of prices. The epidemic of 1558–9 is normally given as an instance of such a correlation: as a consequence of exceptionally high mortality, prices actually fell during the late 1550s and early 1560s. The whole sequence of events during those decades is worthy of consideration for it shows that the historian of the price rise cannot depend upon any mono-causal explanation for its occurrence.

The view was once held that the great debasements of the currency which took place under Henry VIII, Edward VI and Protector Somerset, were to a large extent responsible for the general price rise. When the quantity-of-money theory was challenged, this 'debasement' explanation was also rejected. Recently, however, Dr R. B. Outhwaite has suggested that it contains a good deal of truth. The initial objection was that there is no exact correlation between the dates of the debasements of the coinage (which took the form of a reduction in the amount of silver contained in each coin) and the price rises during the 1540s and early 1550s, and that all prices did not rise to the same degree. This has been countered by several persuasive arguments: that insufficient attention has been paid by critics of the debasement theory to the time lapse between the instructions for debasement and their actual implementation; that historians have failed to realise that other factors acted in conjunction with monetary causes to alter prices; that for some time both debased, pure and foreign coins were in circulation concurrently; that prices would in no circumstances rise uniformly because demand was not uniform and was liable to change *vis-à-vis* different commodities during any given period. These objections make it clear that the lack of an exact synchronisation between the orders for debasement of the coinage and price rises is no argument for a lack of causal connection. As a partial explanation for the accelerated inflationary spiral of the period 1547–56 the coinage debasement theory has much to recommend it. It did have an immediate effect upon the exchange rates, resulting in a rising demand for exports and some rise in import prices which had a varying effect on the level of prices on the home market. It proved of great profit to the Crown, increasing royal purchasing power and credit standing and having an inflationary effect via the new heavy outlays on war provision. Despite royal proclamations forbidding the raising of prices after debasement, some simple adjustment of prices to compensate for the reduced value of coins probably took place. There may have been an eagerness to get rid of money, now debased, and to spend capital. This would put pressure upon land, housing and luxury goods rather than upon food. There is no doubt, however, that it is the interaction between the debasement of the coinage and other factors (demographic pressure, the need to supply the troops, the availability of capital) which is important for an explanation of even this short-term price rise. The extent to which the debasement was responsible for a rise in prices, perhaps accentuated by a sudden increase in silver availability affecting import prices, exacerbated the situation by making it more difficult for the poor to obtain food, and as a consequence lowering the resistance of these poorly nourished people to disease. A high rate of mortality resulted, and, as a consequence of considerably reduced pressure upon available resources, there was a short-term lowering of prices.

Historians generally agree that most of the population increase occurred prior to 1650. There is some doubt about what happened in the late seventeenth century: a slow rise, stagnation or actual decline. It is believed that there were marked regional differences in the growth rate —either because of contrasts in the vital rates of births and deaths or because of the effects of migration (internal emigration and immigration patterns), generally termed 'migration rates'. In the west, north and north-east there is evidence of a marked and sustained excess of burials over births in the late seventeenth century. In the Midlands, on the other hand, population growth recovered its sixteenth-century momentum in this period. For various reasons the Home Counties also witnessed population increase, probably a migration increase rather than a natural one. The overall impression is, however, one of slackening growth and it may be shown that this trend had its own impact upon the movement of prices.

It is true that by the mid-seventeenth century the effect of increased supplies of American silver upon European prices was much diminished, but an explanation of lowered grain prices over the long term in terms of reduced demographic pressure and relatively increased agricultural production is more satisfactory. There was at this time both increased agricultural capacity and a slower rate of increase in the demand for food. The period of the early Stuarts had seen the addition of half a million acres of arable land through fen drainage projects alone and, by the second half of the century, new farming techniques and new crops were becoming more common and better established. At last supply was beginning to meet demand. A reduction in the labour-force appears to have forced real wages upwards to some extent. More of the population had an income surplus as a result (and more were employed) and most devoted this to industrial and luxury items. What pressure there was on prices, therefore, was in the industrial sector and it is here that price rises are to be noted.

### *Demographic patterns*

As has been shown, it is demonstrable that demographic pressure did affect the movement of prices and it is also possible to relate short-term fluctuations in the population growth to variations in prices. The argument concerning the effect of debasement upon prices indicates that the historian can hope to show no more than a general correlation between one factor and another because of the interaction of several different factors at any one time. The historian, however, has a natural wish to do more than simply show that the price and population curves are generally related. He wants to refine his knowledge of demographic factors to show why the population was increasing in the sixteenth and seventeenth centuries and why the rate of growth was not consistent either over the whole period or between one period and another. He also wants to explore demographic patterns for what they may tell us about the development of early modern society along specific lines.

Already the terms 'vital rates' and 'migration rates' have been mentioned. Vital rates are the rates of births and deaths in a society, which when compared tell the historian the rate of natural increase or decline. Migration rates are rates of immigration and emigration: in a study of a given community the difference between the two rates can tell a great deal about the health of the society involved—whether it is dynamic and proving a great attraction to outsiders, or the exact opposite. The first thing the historian must remember when dealing with vital rates is that he rarely, if ever, has direct evidence of these. In western Europe, from the sixteenth century onwards, what he has are baptismal and burial registrations for the most part, which are one step removed from the necessary vital statistics. The registrations, even when complete, are especially suspect where a society contains a large number of persons who do not conform to the established church of the region. In sixteenth- and seventeenth-century England, for example, popish recusants were not entitled to burial in consecrated ground; recusant parents often neglected to bring their children to the established church for baptism. Of course, recusancy was a relatively minor problem in England and Wales, except in the north, but by the late seventeenth century Protestant nonconformity had reached significant proportions and for this reason parish registers, even when complete in other respects, do not provide coverage of the whole local population. Migration rates also must be treated with caution: evidence of excessive migration may be explicable in other than economic terms. For example, there was a large-scale emigration of Huguenots from France in 1685 which occurred as a direct result of Louis XIV's revocation of the Edict of Nantes, which may have had some economic motivation admittedly, but the emigration itself cannot be attributed to lack of economic dynamism in the French urban communities where the Huguenots clustered.

Despite the difficulties involved in establishing true vital and migration rates some valuable research has been undertaken in recent years, following the example of French historical demographers. The Cambridge Group for the History of Population is carrying out an intensive analysis of the parish registers of England and Wales which is involving the establishment of vital rates as well as more detailed studies arising from family reconstruction and resulting information on family size, household size, age-structure, sex-structure, fertility rates, family limitation, geographical (and presumably social) mobility, age at marriage, rates of remarriage, and the effects of epidemic, famine, persecution and urbanisation upon community size. Interim reports on certain aspects of the research have already been published but the project is a long-term one and only in its initial stages as yet. Nevertheless, enough has emerged from these and other studies for historians to formulate some hypotheses about demographic patterns in early modern society.

Vital rates were subject to many different influences. During the late 1550s, the 1580s and 1590s, and the 1620s, for example, bad harvests and epidemics increased the rate of mortality and resulted in a decline in population size. This was a short-term alteration of the prevailing pattern because it implied no reduction in the birth rate. Moreover, it is probable that the plagues and epidemics endemic at this time left children and youth relatively unscathed, thus altering the age balance of the affected community in favour of these groups. For various reasons, population might well recover its losses more rapidly in the years following such a disaster. There was more food to go round—the death rate might actually decline relative to the birth rate as a consequence and fertility rates might improve. More young people would inherit property and feel able to marry and set up homes of their own, and produce offspring. According to the assumption of the eighteenth-century clergyman, Thomas Malthus, that population will expand to meet the limits of available resources, this was a perfectly natural process.

Whether it really occurred in this way, though, is open to question. It is true that certain pieces of research support such an interpretation. D. E. C. Eversley analysed the response of several Worcestershire villages to the epidemic onslaught of 1725–9, which resulted in a huge excess of burials over births and, even, in an immediate decline in registered baptisms because of mortalities among pregnant women and prospective mothers. Immediately after the epidemic, however, there was an increase in the number of marriages and the crude birth rate rose to 42 per thousand or more. Even so, however, it took a quarter of a century to recover the position of 1725. In other cases, for instance that of Colyton, there seems to have been no check of fertility in response to rising prices and no sudden increase in fertility in the period immediately following an epidemic and high mortality, but rather a decline in the birth rate in these post-crisis years. This has been interpreted as a delayed Malthusian response: some historians believe that people were well aware of the pressure of population upon prices and manipulated family size by deliberate limitation to ease their economic circumstances, even though they were not always able to respond quickly enough to the economic situation. Such a view is supported by the fact that there was a direct correlation between class and wealth status of the family and the number of children. Families of the gentry might have an average of two more children than farming families and three or four more than labouring families.

This leads the historian directly to consider what is known about marriage in early modern Britain for it is certain that marriage patterns had a profound impact upon family size and upon the ability of a community to recover and extend its size after a catastrophe. Firstly, demographic historians have come to believe in the prevalence of the European marriage pattern. In western Europe couples were encouraged to be economically independent of their other relatives. It was generally accepted that a man would not get married unless he could ensure a home and livelihood for his wife and family. The age at marriage was, therefore, dependent upon economic self-sufficiency. A surprisingly high average age at marriage prevailed in the sixteenth and seventeenth centuries—of men, 26; of women, 24. There were, however, class differences in the age at marriage—high-born persons being financially able to marry at an earlier age, particularly as the extended family (where several generations dwelt together) more commonly occurred amongst such classes. The recent study of the rural community of Myddle in Shropshire by Dr David Hey rather contradicts the assumption that marriage had to wait until a young man could inherit family property from his father, although he confirms the relatively late age of marriage. Dr Hey cites examples of newly-weds who went to live in other parishes until they inherited property. Obviously, the historian must await further detailed research of this kind before coming to hard and fast conclusions. If Dr Hey's suggestions are borne out, however, many of Dr Peter Laslett's views on the generation gap in Stuart England would be open to question.

It has been shown by several historians that the age at marriage might substantially affect the possible number of children born to a couple, without the necessity of deliberate family limitation. The age of women at marriage is therefore of crucial importance to the demographer. A difference of two years or slightly more might be expected to make a difference of two births because the level of fertility in the first years of marriage was higher than later on. Earlier death amongst married women might have a less dramatic demographic effect than later marriage. It is presumed that the average marriage might yield eight births, although in fact a figure of six is more generally applicable.

As Peter Laslett has shown, however, the death rate and, more particularly, the life expectation of the population could have its own effect upon marriage patterns and upon population growth even when there was no great surplus of deaths over births. He calculated that the average man in the seventeenth century might expect a married life of twenty-five years if he first married at the age of 26. In a rural community it might well be that his son could not marry until he inherited his father's property. Thus the age at marriage quickly became fixed to the life-expectation of the male population. Such a situation had profound effects: it was unlikely that many fathers in certain classes ever lived to see their grandchildren, much less to converse or live with them. In the case of a rural community this could reverberate in several ways. The extended (multi-generational) family was unlikely to be usual—perhaps 1 in 10,000 families were extended, the rest nuclear. A society which basically relied upon oral traditions was in the peculiar position of having a first-hand memory of only one generation. The generations were clearly demarcated. There was also an imbalance in the age-structure of society, very different from that in modern Europe—there was a far higher proportion of young people. The picture has to be modified in certain respects, however. Firstly, the concept of the average is a dangerous one—there were young marriages even among the poor and landless; there were old men; there were old men who saw their grandchildren and even their great-grandchildren. The concept of the median—the point beyond which there were as many as there were below—is more helpful to the historian. Secondly, although it was relatively unusual for men in certain classes of society to reach the age of 70, nevertheless this age was regarded as the natural life span. Thirdly, as aforementioned, it was perfectly possible for the pattern to change, if, for example, there was a sudden reduction in life-expectancy or if a great many men were cut off by epidemic before their sons had reached the usual age for marriage and independence. Also, there has been an assumption that a man married but once during his life. In reality there were many second marriages. Although there was a natural surplus of males at birth this gave way to an excess of girls over men in young adulthood, meaning that there were many young spinsters. However, deaths through childbirth and other causes meant that there was an opportunity for most women to marry.

It would be wrong to leave the reader with the impression that marriage patterns and birth rates were entirely dependent upon economic factors, be they the age of death of the parent, or the availability of financial means. Even in a rural community many men found a source of employment and livelihood which was independent of the parental household or subsequent inheritance of land, although it is true that the system of apprenticeship in most of the established crafts and trades did restrict the age at which independence was achieved and at which marriage was feasible in much the same way. Dr Laslett has also made the interesting point that most young women of the period did not reach the age of menstruation until they were 18, 19 or 20 years old. This fact was partially attributable to diet and there seems to have been a discrepancy between the classes in this regard—well-born girls reached puberty before members of the poorer classes. If girls were physically immature until their late teens and early twenties it is no wonder that young marriages were much less common in early modern England than they are today.

### *Conclusion*

This section has illustrated that knowledge of demographic trends is vital to an understanding of basic economic issues—not only of the price rise itself but also of such matters as the growth of urban communities; mobility; agricultural expansion; internal trade; and social friction. Moreover, however difficult it is even to chart a general population curve for the period, it is not sufficient for the historian to deal only in generalisations. He must know why the rate of growth fluctuated in time and in space. This tells him more about the interaction of economic factors with demographic change—the picture of society becomes ever more complex but, emphatically, it also becomes much richer.

# 2

# Urban Growth in the Provinces

The growth of the metropolis and the course of England's overseas trade have attracted the attention of many historians. The population of London, including the City, Westminster and the near suburbs, had stood at approximately 50,000 in the time of Henry VIII; it had swollen to a quarter of a million by the early seventeenth century. London's growth to a great extent grew out of her advantages in trade with the Continent. In the mid-sixteenth century 90 per cent of England's export trade was dependent upon the cloth industry, and most cloth was exported to Antwerp. Yet although London accommodated one-twentieth of England's population by 1600, she was not the only urban centre in the country, although by far the largest.

There were approximately 810 market towns in England and Wales in the sixteenth century (760 in England; 50 in Wales). These towns varied greatly in size and character. Some were so small that the epithet 'town' was a courtesy title even then—communities of 300 to 400 persons, with a market which served a restricted, local hinterland and a social structure which resembled that of a village. Much more common were towns of between 600 and 2,000 people. Staffordshire, for example, had six such centres—Burton-on-Trent, Stafford, Lichfield, Newcastle, Tamworth and Wolverhampton. These towns had a wider influence, but they still served a local rather than a regional hinterland. Their character was urban, however. Some counties boasted shire towns, having a population in the thousands, traditions of independence, and an enormous economic and social influence over a whole region. The social structure of the shire town was complex and urban. By 1662 there were sixty provincial towns with an average population each of 6,000 to 7,000: clearly these constituted centres not only for the marketing of consumables but also for their consumption. The south-eastern counties contained a number of rival towns in this category. Kent, for instance, had Maidstone and Canterbury; Hampshire had Winchester and Southampton; and Sussex had Chichester and Lewes. All market towns were involved in the distribution of goods brought in from rural areas by farmers and of goods manufactured by craftsmen, but only a very few were also consumers of such goods on a significant scale. In order to function as a market, a town required an official charter. There is evidence, however, that other towns held unofficial markets and fairs, although their existence must have been brief and uncertain.

Why were there so many market towns? Why did they differ in character? Why were urban communities growing in the sixteenth and seventeenth centuries? The first two questions may be answered to some extent by looking at the structure of internal trade in England and Wales during the period and before, and by considering the origins of the urban communities themselves.

Until the sixteenth century agriculture was specialised to no significant extent—although no area was wholly self-sufficient and the subsistence economy has been over-stressed by historians, it is yet true that most of a man's needs were supplied from within his own area, although not from his own farm. Surplus produce was employed in direct or indirect exchange in order to procure other goods. Farming for profit was unusual in the village community. Market centres grew up as the most convenient means of distributing produce [4]. A farmer went to the local market to sell his surplus and with the proceeds buy other produce. As a result of this system, the markets themselves were unspecialised—all manner of available consumable and manufactured goods produced within its hinterland were sold. Difficulties of transportation and preservation of goods limited the extent to which produce from outside areas penetrated the market's region. Market centres, therefore, grew up at frequent intervals. The ideal distance between these local markets would have been about eight to ten miles, allowing the farmer ample time to travel to and from market and conduct his business there within one day. In fact, this ideal distribution did not prevail. In the east a man would live, on average, six miles from the local market; in the Midlands, he would normally live over ten miles away. This difference between regions reflects several factors—there were fewer markets in the north, Midlands and west than in the southern and eastern counties, just as there was a sparser population. Naturally enough, the hinterlands of the various markets were not mutually exclusive—farmers were often able to attend two or three markets which were within easy travelling distance.

If it is reasonably easy to explain why there was such a proliferation of markets, it is a more complex matter to answer why the towns involved differed so in character. Most of the markets were of ancient origin, and had been established by the end of the thirteenth century. The incidence of the Black Death had heralded the demise of scores of market towns which were never to be revived: it has been estimated that the 810 markets of Tudor England and Wales represent but a third of the number in existence before 1349. Norfolk, which had once boasted 130 market centres, now had but 31. Some markets such as Tutbury and Brewood in Staffordshire were verging on extinction in the sixteenth century. This century, however, saw the expansion and prosperity of most market towns and several new markets obtained charters, such as Stevenage in Hertfordshire and Aynho in Northamptonshire. A new or revived market could prosper, either where there were few competitors or where its own superior organisation and geographical advantages worked in its favour.

### *Agricultural change and specialised production*

Two factors, apart from differences in origin, help to explain the varied character of England's towns: agricultural change and growth of population. The sixteenth century witnessed the start of a process of specialisation both in agricultural production and in the marketing of produce. The processes of enclosing, engrossing, fen drainage, floating of water meadows, and introduction of convertible husbandry have already been mentioned. By 1500 certain English counties were already enclosed—Suffolk, Essex, Hertfordshire, Kent, Devon, Somerset, Cornwall, Shropshire, Worcestershire and Herefordshire. In the sixteenth century it was the Midland counties which saw most enclosing activity—Leicestershire, Warwickshire and Northamptonshire. This resulted from the new pressure upon grazing land: more farmers wanted to keep sheep or dairy animals, or simply to enlarge their farming enterprises; there was a need to supply a rapidly growing population and to produce food for the inhabitants of towns, who were agriculturally non-productive. As the Midland shires were, by contemporary standards, areas of dense rural population, there was resistance to enclosure. While not wishing to exaggerate the social ills associated with enclosure and engrossing—chiefly depopulation—it is true that the livelihood of some was jeopardised and that landless labourers turned to the local towns for work when labour demands on the farms were diminished. The rise in population itself put pressure upon land availability and more people had to look outside agriculture for employment. The local towns offered the best prospects. Immigrants became apprenticed to various crafts and trades; others became domestic servants, opened alehouses and inns; still others could find no employment.

The new specialisations in agricultural production, although never total in any one area, greatly affected the character of the markets. Bearing in mind that a large market town might have multiple specialities and that the specialities might vary in some towns according to the time of year, it is possible to trace the pattern of specialisation in English market towns. Over 300 of the markets (more than a third) specialised in the marketing of a specific product. There were more corn markets than any other (133), some 92 cattle markets, 32 sheep markets, 30 fish markets, 30 wool markets and over 27 cloth markets. The hinterlands served by the various markets differed widely, therefore. For instance, corn markets, except in the north, rarely served an area of more than 5 miles radius while wool and cloth markets served an area generally in excess of 20 miles and often of 40 miles radius. The distribution of the different types of market also varied geographically; a third of the corn markets were in the corn-growing areas of the eastern counties; one-third of the cattle markets were in the grazing lands of the Midlands, a quarter in the west and a fifth in the north; wool and cloth markets clustered in the west, north and East Anglia. Economic concentration was evident. The smallest markets, ports and fairs lost agricultural traffic to the larger provincial centres such as Maidstone, Newcastle, King's Lynn and Canterbury. These towns owed their growing prosperity and size to geographical factors—adequate roads; navigable rivers; topographical suitability of the market-place itself which had to be sufficiently large to allow expansion; the extensive and varied character of the town's hinterland. Absence of such advantageous features might well curtail the growth of a town: the failure of Leicester to become a provincial centre has been attributed to her lack of a navigable river, which greatly restricted the hinterland from which she could draw goods and buyers. Other market towns developed from being mere distributive centres into expanding manufacturing towns. Geographical placement was again all-important and a town had to be of sufficient size initially to attract immigrant labour.

*Topography*

In a short chapter it is not possible to detail the growth of every market town in England or of every industrial centre. Recently Dr Alan Dyer has published an excellent study of the city of Worcester in the Tudor period. This does much to explain how Worcester's topography determined the manner in which her citizens lived. The river Severn, then navigable from Bristol to Shrewsbury, made Worcester an important inland port on this commercial route as well as a communications centre on the route connecting Wales with the Midlands and south-east and roads between north and south. The flourishing market and fairs were a reflection of the city's importance as a produce exchange—serving its immediate prosperous region as well as the far wider hinterland of pastoral highlands and arable lowlands. The specialised products of these contrasted areas focused on Worcester. Undoubtedly the city's prosperity was strengthened by an extremely vigorous broadcloth industry, her position as a shire town, and by the fact that she was the administrative centre of the large diocese of Worcester.

The position of Lincoln, centre of a diocese yet larger, was far less favourable. The county was isolated, with appalling roads, no established postal service, and no navigable route to the Midlands and south, despite the fact that the low-lying land was frequently flooded. Projects to reopen the Fossdyke, a canal linking the Witham at Lincoln with the Trent, had a chequered history because of financial difficulties in the second and third decades of the sixteenth century and opposition of the gentry in the 1620s and 1630s. The seventeenth century saw increased demand by the clothing towns of the West Riding for the long wool of Lincolnshire sheep. Lincolnshire had no wool market and this deficiency worked to Lincoln's disadvantage because most of the wool was bought privately by travelling brokers. The Fossdyke could have provided the necessary water transport to make a Lincoln wool market feasible. A project of improvement was first mentioned in 1616 by certain of the county's notables. The Privy Council approved the expenditure of £3,000 to open the channel. The undertaking progressed and collections were begun. There was, however, considerable conflict with the landed interest who wanted to keep water levels low, not raise them. Work began eventually but the project finally foundered in the 1630s. It would be some time before the city could reap the benefits of distributing the county's chief product.

When the importance of navigable water to an urban community was so great, it is small wonder that a city such as Worcester bitterly resisted the planned canalisation of the Warwickshire Avon in the 1630s, fearing that Worcester's pre-eminent position as distributing centre would be jeopardised [5].

### *The effects of occupational structure*

The socio-economic structures of the larger provincial towns varied enormously. Some towns were almost entirely dominated by a single trade or manufacture. In Worcester, for instance, 40 per cent of a sample of self-employed tradesmen between 1540 and 1589 were involved in the cloth trade; the percentage rose to 50 per cent in the period 1590 to 1620. By contemporary standards, this meant that Worcester was highly industrialised. Dr Dyer has suggested that 'any English provincial town with the rudiments of an urban character' possessed an occupational structure in which some 35 to 40 per cent of the employed were engaged in the cloth, food-and-drink, and building trades. Even Coventry, at the height of her importance as a textile town in the 1520s, had only a third of her work-force engaged in the cloth trade. Norwich, another important cloth town, had only 17 per cent of workers involved in the trade.

Worcester's entire economy was dependent upon the fortunes of the cloth trade. The most important groups engaged in the distributive trades there were the mercers, the drapers and the haberdashers. The distributive trades, however, were eclipsed by the end of the 1620s—the percentage engaged in them had been reduced from 13 to 3 per cent, a drop attributable to some extent to the falling-off of rural custom as the rural gentry turned to London for luxury items and as rural areas provided their own weavers and tailors. The Worcester broadcloth industry, with no local competition, specialised in making high-quality cloth. It is possible that by the 1560s Worcester was the largest surviving textile town. The trade was organised on an independent craftsman basis. The industry was controlled both by Act of Parliament (Acts regulated the weight of cloth in 1533, 1551, and 1557) and by city authority and guild intervention. Quality control was enforced: the Act of 1551 gave the city a monopoly of the highest-quality export cloth, but made the price of Worcester broadcloths uncompetitive; the Act of 1557 reduced the weight of cloths and made the price competitive once more. The trade guilds made determined efforts to enforce seven-year apprenticeship.

The reduction in importance of the distributive trades in the city's economy increased the relative value and importance of the cloth trade. However, the cloth trade was peculiarly prone to boom and slump during the period. There had been a temporary, if dramatic, slump in 1557; the 1590s heralded a new wave of prosperity which lasted until the marked slump of the 1620s. An economy which depended to such a great extent upon a single industry could not be secure, especially when that trade was highly susceptible to changes in the world market. The decline of the city's position as supplier of rural requirements added to the economic difficulties. It was the city's position as a regional market centre which was to enable Worcester to weather the storm which had flattened other towns overwhelmingly dependent upon cloth.

The occupational structure of Coventry was more varied. While 14 per cent of the workers were engaged in the clothing trade and 33 per cent in the textile industry, some 11 per cent were involved in tanning and associated leather industries and 9 per cent were engaged in the metal crafts. Coventry's days as a great textile centre were numbered but she, at least, had some hedge against the extreme effects of slump. The situation in Leicester was somewhat different. Here only 8½ per cent of the work-force were engaged in textile production, and tailoring, metal and building accounted for but 22 per cent between them, but some 19 per cent were involved in the leather industry and a high proportion of the butchers in the town were probably more interested in providing hides for the tanners than food for the bellies of inhabitants. The large number of butchers in Leicester (27 in all) raised the percentage involved in the food-and-drink trades to 21 per cent (as against 15 in Northampton and 15½ in Coventry and circa 12 in Worcester) whereas Leicester's current population of approximately 3,000 scarcely warranted such a number.

*The economic consequences of a guild structure*

Some historians have claimed that the economies of many British towns suffered because the trades clung to their medieval guild structures, failing to adapt to the trading requirements of a new age. Dr David Palliser's study of the trade guilds of Tudor York contests this view. York's size and importance had dwindled considerably since the early fifteenth century. A population of perhaps 12,000 in 1500 had dwindled to 8,000 by the middle of the century; the city's relative size, too, had decreased —York had stood second in 1334 (according to taxable wealth) but stood fourteenth in 1523–4. This marked change in the city's size and wealth was attributable to a decline in the textile industry between 1450 and 1550: the city's recovery as a regional capital after that date was due less to a cloth revival than to transport improvements, York's importance as a social centre, and the establishment of both the King's Council of the North and the Ecclesiastical Commission in the city during the Elizabethan and early Stuart periods. Yet there was a simultaneous recovery in trade, dependent to a great extent upon these new conditions, which deserves attention. Within the city there was a freemen's trading monopoly. Those wishing to trade in the city were required to attain the status of freemen by apprenticeship, purchase or inheritance, a rule which was in force elsewhere [6]. Nearly half the adult male population of York were freemen. Only freemen were entitled to guild membership. York boasted around 51 craft guilds in 1485; several disappeared in the following years but new guilds were authorised which took their place; by 1579 there were some 64 guilds. The most important were the Society of Merchant Adventurers (mercers, merchants, grocers, apothecaries, spicers); the drapers and tailors (who united in 1551–2); and the haberdashers, felters and cappers (who joined in 1591). A great many of England's larger towns had a very similar pattern of guild organisation, with these three groups dominant. There were also a number of handicraft guilds. The textile industry and the textile guilds as a consequence were faring badly in the face of West Riding competition. In 1561 the York Corporation claimed that there were only ten poor weavers in the entire city; the weavers' guild survived because of the existence of linen weaving, but other textile guilds, such as the walkers' and cardmakers', disappeared shortly after 1529. York's importance as a textile distribution centre, however, is reflected in the fact that the tailors' guild was next in importance and size to the Merchant Adventurers.

The government of the guilds was conducted by men anxious to preserve the strength and vitality of the constituent trades. Of prime importance was the regulation of apprenticeship. Minimum apprenticeship terms of six and then seven years were already the norm in York by 1530, when masters taking on apprentices for less than seven years were fined. In 1574 the founders' guild went even further than the national legislation of 1563 by ordering terms of eight years. In the fifteenth century it had been common to order that no master should take more than one or two apprentices simultaneously. During the period 1520–60, corresponding with York's economic slough, such restrictions were lifted, but the return to prosperity in the 1560s saw the renewal of limited recruitment. Elizabeth's reign saw a rise of only 17 per cent in the intake of freemen, but a rise of 63 per cent in the number of men becoming freemen by inheritance occurred. As a result, freemen were anxious that new recruits should not oust the freemen's sons from their rights and opportunities. The regulation of apprenticeship ensured control over standards and numbers: it is but one example of the way in which the guilds, still vigorous and meaningful, adapted themselves to new economic and social conditions.

Moreover, in York the guilds were closely supervised by the Corporation. Quarrels and abuses were checked; wages controlled; standards of production kept high; competition encouraged; new trades sponsored; monopolies supervised. Dr Palliser cites the example of the bakers' guild which possessed a monopoly and was often accused of abusing its position. For much of the 1540s and 1550s the Corporation permitted competition from a group called the 'boll bakers', part-time bakers within the city, and some country bakers. The bakers' monopoly was restored only on condition that they sell bread at lower rates than those charged by their rivals. The Common Council of the guilds themselves played some part in city government and was particularly active in promoting market reform. There is thus no evidence that the guilds of Tudor York were anachronistic—they were vigorous and alive to the subtleties of the city's economic life; the guild structure was not responsible for keeping away new industry; as a system it was 'able to survive intact precisely because there was so little industry there to conflict with it'.

*The ports*

This chapter has emphasised the development of the inland provincial towns, which played a prominent role in internal trade. Yet England's largest cities were the ports—coastal ports such as London, Bristol, Exeter, King's Lynn, Hull and Newcastle. The development of the ports, other than London, followed a distinctive pattern. The rate of growth of individual ports was affected by the state of trade, the development of regional specialities, and the ability of merchants to procure exportable goods and the necessary investment. In the early sixteenth century exports of woollen cloth and barley and wheat were the most significant. The trade in grain exports reached a peak in the period 1570–1600 and saw a decline under the early Stuarts. Between 1500 and 1640 grain farming became dominant in the eastern counties. There was a simultaneous rise in exports of grain, which found an outlet through the Norfolk ports of King's Lynn and Great Yarmouth. More than 80 per cent of the grain passed through these two ports: by the seventeenth century it is probable that at least 60 per cent of the entire country's grain exports were being handled by King's Lynn and Great Yarmouth. The prospective destination of most of the country's grain favoured these ports: most was intended for the Netherlands, for the markets of Antwerp and other cities on the Scheldt; for Amsterdam and other Dutch towns. King's Lynn's exports totalled 180 quarters in 1509, reaching a peak of 20,000 quarters in 1588–9. A more restricted market for grain exports in Rouen and other cities of northern and western France bought trade to the Sussex and Kentish ports; demand from Spain was answered by exports from Bristol, Bridgwater and Bideford, although this trade fluctuated in pace with Henry VIII's matrimonial enthusiasms, the state of Elizabeth's foreign policy, and the uncertainty of early Stuart relations with Spain.

London, of course, was predominant in the cloth trade but the ports of Hull and Newcastle competed effectively in exporting cloth to the Baltic. Newcastle was also a busy centre for the shipping of coal around the coast and her trade increased in importance during the seventeenth century. Expansion of the shipping industry and the concentration of the export trade in certain ports gave rise to a number of commercial and industrial supportive enterprises. The growing ship-building industry of

London, East Anglia and of the coastal region between Hull and Newcastle is perhaps the most noteworthy. Ancillary industries such as sail and rope making and joinery were also stimulated. Imports also provided commercial opportunities for the ports. Some of the larger ports boasted merchant communities: Bristol had 150 merchants in 1600 out of a population of circa 12,000. Several of the western ports were profiting from the Newfoundland fishing industry in the seventeenth century, especially Bristol and Plymouth. The important city of Exeter, on the other hand, relied for its wealth upon the western production of woollen cloth.

It is small wonder, then, that 'in the first division of the urban league table were seven or eight major cities' all but one ports, which numbered by the end of the seventeenth century London, Norwich, Bristol, Exeter, York, Newcastle-upon-Tyne and Hull. By 1700 all had populations in excess of 8,000. By 1640 Exeter had already a population of 9,000 to 10,500. York's population rose from 8,000 to 12,000 in a century. By 1700 both Bristol and Norwich had populations of above 20,000. In singling out these great coastal and inland ports, the historian should not forget the claims of a rapidly growing 'second division'—Plymouth, grown rich on the profits of war, boasted a population of 8,000 to 9,000 in the early 1640s and regional centres and inland ports such as Worcester (already over 6,000 in the sixteenth century) and Canterbury (6,000 in 1640) were expanding as marketing, administrative and social centres.

### *The regional centre*

The economic historian, while aware of the importance of trade and industry to the life of towns, should not neglect those aspects of urban life associated with the towns' positions as regional social, political, educational and professional centres. The case of York well illustrates the economic side of these aspects. Large and small provincial towns alike served their hinterlands in other than economic ways. The school in the local market town might be the only securely established school in the area. Doctors, apothecaries, lawyers (both ecclesiastical and common law), and teachers focused on the towns. The county town gradually became an important meeting-place for the country gentry. Major inns, such as the Star at Maidstone, responded by becoming social centres. According to Professor Alan Everitt they 'began to assume the functions of a county hall, where the gentry foregathered to discuss the news of the shire, resolve its administrative problems, and air its grievances'. Naturally such activity was most important when the courts were in session or when markets and fairs were taking place, because these acted as magnets to the county notables. Nevertheless, towards the close of Elizabeth's reign some county gentry were already having town houses built. The lawyers who proliferated in Tudor and Stuart England found a clientele easily—they were instrumental in the land transactions of gentry and yeomen alike; they drew up the bonds necessary in private bargaining. The increasing social prestige of the professions helped consolidate in its turn the social position of the town. This was a foretaste of the situation in the late seventeenth and eighteenth centuries when the 'season in town' became both fashionable and customary among the county 'quality'.

The social and economic consequences of these developments were legion. On the one hand the consolidation of professional, middle-class and gentry communities within the town brought work for the already growing building trade. Natural increase in the population, immigration, and the pattern of nuclear rather than extended households undoubtedly gave a tremendous boost to this trade. Demand for more luxurious dwellings by immigrant gentry and professionals was yet more profitable. A substantial rise in numbers in the building industry appears to have occurred in Worcester during the years 1540–1620. Between 1540 and 1640 the population doubled, the growth rate steadily accelerating. Two-thirds of the increase may be attributed to the excess of baptisms over burials (with increased birth rate in the late sixteenth century giving way to decreased infant mortality in the seventeenth), and one-third to immigration. Of course, a large number of the immigrants were apprentices or domestic servants who would lodge with their masters, but the increase in potential householders was very significant. As early as the 1520s 7½ per cent of Northampton's work-force, 4½ per cent of Coventry's, and 4 per cent of Leicester's were involved in the building trade.

The presence of the professional classes and gentry in the town also created a demand for luxury goods and food and drink. Where these classes favoured a town, either as inhabitants or frequent visitors, they to some extent compensated for the disappearance of the other great consumers, the religious houses and wealthy ecclesiastics. The decline of Coventry was attributed by Dugdale in 1656 to the loss of her religious houses. Seats of dioceses and regional or shire towns had a natural advantage when it came to developing as social or administrative centres. Ilchester in Somerset, decaying as a market centre, nevertheless held its own in the early seventeenth century because both the County Court and Quarter Sessions met there and because it held the county gaol. Similarly, Chard attracted immigrant customers when the Assizes were held there. Wells's position was more secure. Clergy, ecclesiastical lawyers and a 'quasi-gentry polite society' clustered into the Cathedral liberty. Bath, already famous for its waters, had become more fashionable and cosmopolitan than any other Somerset town. Prominence as a market centre, therefore, was not always the chief criterion for development as a successful social centre.

The food-and-drink trades of the towns were growing rapidly in response both to the demands of the permanent population and to the needs of itinerant tradesmen, brokers, farmers and others. The extent of their growth depended upon the economic structure of the town concerned. In Worcester, highly industrialised and with few agricultural producers, the food-and-drink trades were relatively more important than in many rural towns. Innkeepers and alehouse keepers everywhere in the city boomed. In 1590 in Worcester there was an alehouse per every 100 head of population.

Both inns and alehouses were social centres and the inns situated on the major trade routes, in particular, played an important role in the development of new systems of private marketing during the period. The traditional open market system, carefully regulated by the governments of market towns, was under acute pressure. A whole community of factors and drovers came into being to serve the needs of the expanding London market, searching the provinces for cattle, corn and fruit. The impact of London's growth on the provinces must not be exaggerated—relatively London was expanding much faster than the rest of the country, but the absolute growth of London was much smaller than that of the country as a whole. Yet the impression which London's expansion made upon certain regions was great—for instance, upon the market-gardening pockets of Kent. Simultaneously the effect of royal purveyancing and victualling of large armies had been to increase this population of merchants. When the armies disappeared, the merchants diverted their attentions to the export market and continued to traverse the counties in search of produce. The expansion of the population of certain areas—for example, districts like Tyneside and Staffordshire—was outstripping the ability of local agriculture to meet its demands. Many areas were incapable of expanding production sufficiently. Thus there was a need to import supplies from less densely-populated areas. Annual fairs and private transactions in inns, warehouses and barns by brokers and travellers provided the means for this trade on a national or regional scale, as opposed to the markets which had been designed to distribute local surpluses.

As Professor Everitt has demonstrated, the inns of provincial towns played an integral part in the business of private marketing. Few towns were without an inn; many had several. According to a census of 1577, there were over 1,600 in twenty-five English counties. Yorkshire had 239. By the late seventeenth century, Salisbury could accommodate 548 travellers and 865 horses. Thoroughfare towns, such as Nuneaton or St Albans, possessed many hostelries. William Mosely's inn (one of 30 or more in St Albans) had 21 rooms and far more beds. James I's reign saw the establishment of many inns as specialist marts. Barley was sold at the George Inn in Milton Regis by merchants, maltmen and yeomen from Faversham, Sittingbourne and other towns. It was said that 'thousands of pounds changed hands every Friday' at the Bear Inn, Exeter, one of the town's principal business centres. Clearly the innkeeper was able to influence the pattern of private trading. He could provide warehousing for his clients' goods. Some participated in the trade: John Byde, innkeeper of Keynsham near Bath, was said to buy corn in Warminster, Wiltshire, in order to resell it in Bristol. Most, however, restricted their activities to helping their patrons sell goods. They helped to initiate negotiations for sale, provided the services of the local scrivener in drawing up bonds, and supposedly encouraged fair dealing.

*The nature of urban growth and its problems*

The diverse patterns of development of English provincial towns owed much to topographical situation, occupational structure, population size, political and administrative requirements, and the marketing demands of locality and region. The historian is interested also in the nature of urban growth and its attendant problems. As already indicated, the expansion in Britain's urban population derived from two sources: natural increase and immigration. Studies of geographical mobility, and particularly of immigration into towns, are increasingly popular. It has long been known that apprenticeship acted as a major vehicle of immigration. Apprentices and domestic servants were, however, often very transient immigrants, returning home or travelling elsewhere when they had acquired their training. Apprentices often came from the immediate locality of the town. Whereas 60 per cent of apprentices in Southampton between 1500 and 1700 were from outside the port, their catchment area was largely restricted to Hampshire and its surrounds. Norwich apprentices largely came from Norfolk. The presence of large numbers of apprentices and domestic servants necessarily affected the age-structure of a town. Father Roger Mols has estimated that one-twelfth to one-quarter of a population (particularly in commercial centres) might be composed of household staff. The fact that most of the domestics were female probably balanced the sex-structure which had been unbalanced by the occurrence of so many male apprentices. Perhaps 3 to 7 per cent of the community, however, would consist of male domestic staff.

These two substantial groups of temporary immigrants added to the instability and fluidity of urban population. But there was much immigration into English towns which cannot be accounted for by apprenticeship and service. After a close inspection of Worcester's baptismal and burial registers, Dr Dyer established that one-third of Worcester's population growth during the period was due to immigration from the surrounding countryside. Other towns attracted immigrant workers not only from the immediately surrounding rural areas but from counties far afield. Peter Clark, in his study of migrants in the Kentish towns of Maidstone, Faversham and Canterbury, 1580–1640, has distinguished two groups of immigrants. Betterment migration occurred when people decided to move their dwelling in hope of social or economic improvement and was not normally the result of necessity. Mr Clark suggests that small towns like Faversham (1,000) and Maidstone (2,000) attracted betterment migrants from rural areas within a very small radius of the towns themselves (up to 11 miles) while Canterbury pulled them from a radius of 11 to 15 miles. Apprentices formed an important part of this group. The attraction for many local migrants of migrating to the nearest town was the presence of family connections there who might sponsor their fortunes. Many local migrants maintained physical contact with their previous rural homes and with the families which they left behind. A townsman might return to help with the harvest. Betterment migration was no new phenomenon although the drift to the town seems to have been intensified during this period. Subsistence migration appears to have been a phenomenon peculiar to this period, seeing its true upsurge in Elizabeth's reign. Many of the immigrants into the three Kentish towns came from the county itself. The disafforestation of the Weald and the Downlands, the depopulation of Sheppey and Romney Marsh, and the contraction of the Wealden iron industry impelled many to move towards those maritime towns where growing coastal trade and naval establishments promised employment or, at least, more adequate poor relief. Canterbury and suburbs in 1600 had over 20 relief funds. The confusion of town boundaries and consequent slack administration meant that squatters could remain in towns undetected. However, the rapid expansion of population, the shortage of food, land, and work were national and not merely Kentish problems and consequently many subsistence migrants from outside Kent found their way into these towns—including many demobbed soldiers and sailors. Such immigrants were generally free from family ties, more flexible in their approach to travel, more able to move on at short notice, and more willing to travel long distances in search of work. Within this number of subsistence migrants there was an element of professional roguery, which has been over-emphasised by historians, although it is true that it was all too tempting for the desperate to resort to criminal means. Yet for the most part the migrants in this group were unorganised and unstructured, impelled by the necessity of obtaining food and escaping their unpleasant pasts [7]. In contrast to betterment migration, subsistence migration was largely an urban to urban movement. While only one in three or four of immigrants actually from Kent hailed from an urban environment, the ratio of immigrants from other counties was nearer one in two. A third group of seasonal migrants should also be distinguished—the harvesters.

English towns expanded under the impact of both the betterment and the pauper migrant but one should not forget that emigration from towns also ran at a high level. Not all the emigrants from the three Kentish towns were apprentices: of a sample of 98 emigrants, 63 had been born in one of the towns. There was also a constant flow of migrants from one part of the town to another, crossing parish bounds, drifting to the suburbs. There is evidence that the heavy incidence of pauper migration, possibly actually heightened by the existence of charitable funds designed to relieve the indigenous poor, encouraged epidemic, plague and a high death rate. Vagrants must often have carried infection into overcrowded sectors of towns, where the people were habitually undernourished and susceptible to illness and disease. A third of the population of Norwich was carried off by an epidemic in 1579–80 and during the century the city's population fluctuated wildly between 12,000 and 32,000 because of plague.

Undoubtedly the pauper problem was closely associated with long-distance migration. Worcester, in the period 1540–1640, never had a pauper population in excess of 2 per cent of her total population and private charity and public relief were well able to cope with a problem of this size. For some other towns, more affected by subsistence migrants, the problem achieved more serious dimensions. In 1616, for example, Sheffield was said to have a begging pauper population of 725 (one-third of her total population of 2,207) and an additional 160 persons were so poor that a fortnight's unemployment would reduce them to beggary. Several towns organised censuses of their poor, prior to setting up new systems of poor relief. The Norwich census of 1570 recorded details of 2,300 men, women and children [8]. A surprising number of the poor, one-quarter of the whole, were aged 60 or over. The poor were very dependent upon relief. The men worked in the textile, leather, clothing and building trades. The women, almost twice as numerous as the men, were mainly employed in spinning. The families of the poor were generally small and the children were normally employed in the textile industry. A surprising number of families were willing to sacrifice this income while their children attended industrial or petty schools. 36 of the 69 families which had immigrated to the city were from outside the county —from Suffolk, Essex and the north. As long as these immigrants found employment, it seems that they were not ejected from the city.

Whereas the Elizabethan Poor Laws, encapsuled in the Acts of 1572, 1598 and 1601, primarily concerned themselves with the obliteration or at least suppression of the class of sturdy beggars, local corporations were more advanced. No less concerned with control of the vagabond sector, local legislation catered for the care of the indigenous poor and made far more provision for work for the unemployed. Experiments in poor relief began in London (understandably, as in 1517 the metropolis was said to contain 1,000 deserving beggars and by 1594 almost four times that number) and took the form of grain provision in time of dearth, the refoundation of St Thomas's hospital for the sick and disabled and of Christ's for children of the poor, and the provision of Bethel for the insane and Brideswell for 'sturdy beggars', culminating in the introduction of a compulsory poor-rate in 1547 some 16 years before governmental steps in that direction and 25 years before the Statute of Artificers clearly set out such a central policy. Poor organisation, the allowance of some begging, and the fact that relief was publicly distributed and actually attracted beggars to the capital, all contributed to the partial failure of the scheme. Nevertheless, experiments in London proved useful to the central authorities as demonstrations of the feasibility of such projects and also provided the basis for provincial schemes to deal with the problem of poverty.

Norwich, for example, had established a permanent stock of grain for poor relief by 1558 and cities such as Bristol and Canterbury had experimented in like manner. Lincoln, Ipswich, Norwich, York, Cambridge and Gloucester all followed the metropolitan policy of licensing beggars. Most towns did not initiate schemes until well after the middle of the sixteenth century—it was then that problems arising from rapidly expanding population, rising prices, poor harvests (such as occurred during Edward VI's reign), and the difficulties of the export trade, were making themselves felt. Ipswich modelled its relief scheme directly upon that of London. Cambridge followed suit although there was no attempt to found a town hospital until 1578, whereas Ipswich had a combined house of correction, hospital for the aged and training centre for the young by 1569. York based its system upon three municipally-governed hospitals for the indigent poor. The proceeds of work undertaken by able-bodied paupers went towards relief for the destitute. Lincoln also followed London's example closely. As early as 1543 citizens were forbidden to give unauthorised alms to the poor; by 1547 beggars were licensed and work was to be found for them; after 1551 paupers were bound apprentice to clothiers for eight or nine years. In 1560 an officer was appointed to supervise the care of the poor—an appointment directly modelled upon that of London's Master of Beggars. As Dr Paul Slack has shown, certain towns did not implement relief schemes of their own until the seventeenth century. That of Salisbury, supported by a Puritan clique among the aldermen, in the 1620s was ambitious but short-lived.

Until 1570 Norwich was little affected by the problem of poverty although itinerant beggars proved a nuisance, being normally whipped and expelled from town, and the potential threat from the indigenous poor was realised. Probably the occurrence of the rebellion of the Earls in 1569 spurred the city into action. Mayor John Aldrich, anxious to render the poor politically harmless perhaps, inaugurated the 1570 census and following upon this, drastic action was taken. Begging was totally forbidden and a complete Poor Law organisation was brought into being, supported by a relief rate levied on all inhabitants able to pay. The system survived well into the next century. In the 1570s 950 people were contributing to support 380 regular 'pensioners' and by 1574 the annual relief receipts stood at £530, and remained at £500 for the rest of the decade. In 1565 the Bridewell was opened to house vagabonds. Select women were appointed for the care of the younger children. Some young people were sent to St Giles's hospital for education and training. Increased alms provided for the impotent and aged; work was given to those able to work. A corpus of officials, including the Master of Bridewell, four aldermen in charge of the four administrative areas of the city, and deacons, was set up. The system underwent constant modification and real attempts were made to avoid vagrancy. The scheme was important, not only because of its relative success, but also because it was consistently applied and made the city independent of private charity.

Whereas Dr Laslett may be correct in maintaining that the experience of most Englishmen living in so-called towns was not urban in any real sense, it is clear that some of the larger ports and regional centres were experiencing in miniature the problems of the sprawling metropolis. The nature and extent of urban growth in sixteenth- and early seventeenth-century Britain was varied but the inhabitants of the towns, however small, knew that their life was different in kind from that of their rural neighbours. To expect an early modern town to compare with the industrial sprawl of a nineteenth-century city is to confuse the issue—townsmen may not have been totally divorced from their rural past and may not have experienced an industrialised society but they were no longer countrymen.

# 3

# Education for Society

The study of education is not peripheral but central to an understanding of society. Schools may be in the vanguard of new ideas—about the role of the child in society; about the needs of society and how to fulfil them through education; about the function of education itself, whether as a tool for social control, or as a social leveller, or as a social divider—or they may be the agents of the perpetuation of a conservative society. Contemporary ideas of the function of education found expression in the practice of education itself and it is therefore to the schools, universities and other, more informal, vehicles of education, as well as to works of theory, that one should look to obtain a full picture of the relationship between education and early modern society.

Schools were being set up in many of the Italian city states by the twelfth century but the emergence of institutionalised education in Italy and parts of France was far in advance of that in, for example, England or Germany. The spread of literacy itself seems to have been a fifteenth-century phenomenon in England. The historian, therefore, when studying educational development in England in the period from 1500 to 1660, must look not only at established or emerging schools but also at the educational role of family and church which was being eroded only gradually.

Traditionally the family was regarded as the primary acculturation agent. It introduced the child to society, and taught him the norms of that society and the necessary skills to make his way within it.

The ability of the family to fulfil this function was dependent upon certain conditions. Foremost of these was that the society should be an exceedingly conservative and static one. The parents had to possess the skill which was to be transmitted to the children. In an agrarian society, such conditions normally pertained. Children more often than not followed in the occupational footsteps of their fathers.

In his *Utopia* Thomas More expressed the traditional view when he said, 'Most children are brought up to do the same work as their parents, since they tend to have a natural feeling for it.' But even in the most conservative of societies there had to be some provision for the training of a child who wished to pursue an occupation outside the competence of his parent. 'If a child fancies some other trade, he's adopted into a family that practises it.'

### *Apprenticeship*

Bearing in mind the pressures on the traditional society in early modern Britain it seems natural that more and more children should be requiring a training which their parents were unable to provide, and this in spite of official attempts to reinforce the *status quo* by permitting apprenticeship to certain trades only to children of parents who were not husbandmen or labourers and forcing the children of artificers into their fathers' crafts [9]. Population pressure on land; increasing regional specialisation; the growth of urban communities—all these factors meant that training outside the home became popular and necessary. Apprenticeship and bonded servitude were the common modification of training in the home. A boy or girl was indentured to a master as either servant or apprentice. The formal document specified that the master would command the child's or adolescent's services for a given period according to certain conditions. Most notably, the master was not only to teach the child a specific skill but also to act *in loco parentis*, providing the child with fatherly care and discipline as well as catering for his material needs. In a way incomprehensible to us today the position of child and servant/apprentice was intended to be interchangeable. For a start, servants were normally children or adolescents—apprentices in Southampton, for example, ranged between 3 and 24 years of age—and both their tender years and the system of indenture made them no more masters of their own labour or destiny than were real children of the house. It is essential that one should grasp this fact – apprentices and servants had exchanged one home for another, for there was only a slowly-growing contemporary concept of vocational education outside the family unit.

Apprenticeship was undoubtedly an important vehicle of both geographical and occupational mobility. It was ports such as London, Bristol and Southampton which proved most attractive. 1,449 children were bound apprentice in Bristol in the decade 1532–42. Of these, surprisingly few were bound apprentice to mariners although ropemaking, shipbuilding and ironmongery were trades associated with the life of the port which were well represented. 128 boys were bound apprentice to merchants—more than to any other calling. Trades for which Bristol had a special reputation—wine-trading and tanning, for example—were popular. 91 were apprenticed to hoopers or coopers (makers of barrels); 107

were apprenticed to tanners or colourers of leather; another group were to be trained in saddle-making. The mercers and drapers and the service trades also proved popular. No fewer than 121 youths were seeking to become tailors.

The Southampton apprenticeship registers, 1609–1740, illustrate just how great a factor apprenticeship was in occupational mobility [10]. Slightly above 50 per cent of poor children bound apprentice were entering trades other than those practised by their parents. The pattern was similar among ordinary apprenticeships. Some trades and crafts again made more use of the system than others. Few fishermen and mariners took on boys; brewing, organised on capitalist lines in the port, rarely took on apprentices; but the cloth industry took 40 per cent of Southampton's apprentices, thus making extensive use of the formal system, probably because the industry was still arranged on a domestic, skilled basis. Here, as elsewhere, it is noticeable that the skilled handicraft occupations took a high proportion of the total number of apprentices. Moreover, although apprenticeship provided an opportunity for boys (and girls) to train for occupations other than those practised in the family, there was a marked class bias in the types of trade or craft chosen. Also, few masters took more than one apprentice in a ten-year period.

Although the Statute of Artificers of 1563 had appointed seven years as the minimum period of apprenticeship, the actual period indentured for after 1601 was often much longer. Among the first hundred poor children apprenticed at Southampton in the period 1609–1632, 15 were indentured for 9 years; 18 for 10 years; 5 for 11 years; and 14 for 12 years. The average term was 9.4 for girls and 10 for boys. These agreements were made under the terms of the 1601 Act which empowered overseers of the poor to bind boys to the age of 24 and girls to that of 21 or marriage. The term of apprenticeship for ordinary apprentices was much more ordinarily seven years or only slightly above, particularly because many of the guilds refused to take apprentices beneath a specified age.

Apprentices registered in both poor child and general lists at Southampton were to be maintained by their masters, who normally had to provide food, lodging and, occasionally, full apparel. The indentures stipulated the extent of the master's obligation to instruct the apprentice, normally merely in his master's trade or craft. About the middle of the seventeenth century, however, there was an increasing tendency for indentures, especially of poor girl apprentices, to specify that the child be taught to read and sometimes to write: in the early seventeenth century such obligations were rare. It is probable that because poor children were normally apprenticed at a much earlier age than ordinary apprentices, provision for their instruction in literacy was felt to be more crucial. It would be expected that a youth entering one of the mercantile trades at the age of 14 would already have mastered the rudiments. For the poor child, whose apprenticeship was arranged and financed by the Corporation with charitable funds, apprenticeship truly did involve the substitution of one family environment for another in a much fuller sense than for the adolescent apprentice whose own parents had been able to provide him with preparatory instruction already. Most apprentices received some sort of endowment from their masters on completion of their term. For ordinary apprentices this normally took the form of two sets of clothing and a sum of money which, although rarely adequate to set him up in business, was usually sufficient to equip him with tools of his trade. Poor apprentices fared less well—about 20 per cent of indentures stipulated a final money payment; most mentioned the provision of clothing; a few stated that tools would be found.

The problem of poverty was a serious one but the apprenticeship system was an economically wasteful method of providing for the future of poor children and youth. Corporations took their responsibilities in this respect very seriously. In some years as many as 60 or 70 poor children were apprenticed by the town of Southampton and in the period between 1610 and 1632 approximately 60 per cent of these children were from families of clothworkers, labourers and seamen. Not all were the children of paupers. The children of parents judged incapable of making proper provision for their upbringing were also bound apprentice by town funds. The cost and trouble of making such arrangements was great. Money was given to masters taking on poor apprentices far earlier than the custom of paying premiums became usual in private apprenticeship contracts. Hard bargaining often took place before an agreement was reached. In some cases the Corporation agreed to provide clothing or money in lieu; money payments themselves ranged between three shillings and fourpence and £8 with most falling in the range of ten shillings to £5. Payments tended to be larger if the child was very young. The money was paid in instalments: if the child or master died soon after the indenture was taken out, part of the premium would be repaid; if the child's deceased relatives had left property to endow his apprenticeship, this would be used as a contribution towards the cost. Nevertheless, the system was expensive and time-consuming. Moreover, as time went on the Corporation had to look further and further afield to find masters willing to take poor children.

Several experiments were carried out in various towns to try to make apprenticeship of poor children more economically efficient. Very few masters in Southampton took on more than one apprentice at a time and, basically, these experiments tried to introduce multiple apprenticeship—which resulted in institutions resembling craft or trade schools. At Norwich, for example, poor children were distributed amongst chosen women to learn knitting, weaving and ABC. Flemish influence led to the establishment of a thriving weaving, spinning and knitting school at Canterbury. Christ's Hospital, London, provided craft as well as academic instruction.

Such ideas were given a theoretical basis by the writings of men like Sir William Petty. He would have liked to convert ordinary schools to trade or industrial schools, believing that education should be more closely related to life. In 1647 he recommended the foundation of a technical college and the production of a great textbook of trades which would describe in great detail *all* the different trades, including a full description of the manual operations and the tools used.

While the establishment of craft schools might take the place of individual apprenticeship for some poor children entering occupations with no strong guild organisation, apprenticeship long remained essential for boys entering mercantile trades and skilled occupations, for only by serving a full seven-year term of apprenticeship might a youth gain the freedom of his guild and town and be able to set up in business on his own account. The apprenticeship system was seriously weakened during the Civil War and Interregnum period when demobbed soldiers and sailors were permitted to enter trades for which they had served no apprenticeship term [11]. There were proposals for the abolition of all apprenticeship restrictions. It was not until 1694, however, that the stipulation of the Statute of Artificers debarring the sons of poorer freeholders and copyholders from the clothing industry was repealed. By the beginning of the eighteenth century the system of apprenticeship was beginning to break down.

### *The demand for institutionalised education*

For some time in the sixteenth century, there had been a growing demand for institutionalised education preparatory to apprenticeship. It was only the wealthy and influential who could afford to hire a private tutor or, alternatively, send their children into the household of some other influential man to obtain an education. Lord Burghley's household provided opportunities for a limited number of such boys. By living in his family circle, boys hoped to obtain not only academic instruction but also political, social and financial patronage. Outside this circle of wealthy families there was a growing feeling that children should be taught to read and write, if nothing more, and this led to a demand for educational facilities within the financial means of such families.

On the one hand the roots of this feeling were embedded in the mass literacy movement. Once it was accepted that the majority of the population should be basically literate, the corollary was that schools of one sort or another must be provided to transmit the necessary skills. This was because a very low percentage of the heads of families were themselves literate and in a position to teach their charges. Who should provide the requisite teaching was one crucial issue; why it was felt to be necessary is another.

The spread of literacy was of vital importance to Protestants. Christianity had always had its roots in the Bible but, until the Reformation, popular access to the Bible had been restricted and knowledge of its message conveyed via the priest and chosen imagery, such as stained glass windows, wall pictures, and statues. Protestantism was founded on the conviction that popular familiarity with the Bible message was essential [12]. Because there was no tradition of oral repetition upon which to build (the pre-Reformation Bible had been in Latin) and because the standard of preaching was and was likely to remain abysmally low, the people had to be taught to read. The invention of printing and the availability of cheap paper made this approach viable. Almost half the books published in England in the period 1475–1640 had both a religious purpose and content.

Puritanism had an even more significant effect upon the development both of education and the occupational structure in Britain. Puritans such as William Perkins disagreed with the traditional arrangement whereby children either followed their father's career or the path chosen for them by the parent regardless of aptitude or choice. Perkins believed that each individual was *elect* by God to a particular role in life—be it cleric, lawyer, cobbler, victualler or merchant—and he saw education as giving each child the opportunity to *discover* his calling. In this sense schooling provided a general preparation for life, a chance to find one's feet, to discover one's God-given aptitudes. This involved a reconciliation of the conflicting views of subjective choice of career according to talents espoused by humanists such as Erasmus and that of calling against will and inclination as put forward by Luther and Calvin—the difference being that between choosing and being chosen.

Perhaps of even greater educational and social significance were the views of Richard Greenham. He was very much aware of the impressionability of the child and of the effect, good or bad, of home and school environment. In order to control the development of a child a deliberate policy had to be pursued—the child would inevitably be moulded by environment and experience and, therefore, no education meant a corrupt education. He agreed with Perkins that this deliberate moulding of the child's character by church and school authorities must take account of the individual child's talents.

These views, echoed by many, introduce two or more important elements into the picture. Firstly, the element of choice, but not subjective choice, in career was fostered in practice. Schools might provide some practical, craft training for pupils but they were to serve an entirely different function from apprenticeship. Education was to be on a sufficiently general basis to equip the child for whatever career he seemed intended for. Secondly, education, and particularly education outside the home, was envisaged as a force for good, able to counter the evil influences of family environs and to mould the child's character according to Christian precepts.

Thus we see that popular literacy and formal education were felt by Protestants to be profoundly important. Because traditionally the Church controlled the educational media, and because this interest was in the extension of mass literacy—irrespective of the demands of occupation—this religious motivation is extremely significant.

There were other important reasons for the extension of formal schooling in early modern England. One was, certainly, that more and more jobs required skills which could not be imparted reliably through any other means. The emergence of the printing industry, for instance, meant not only the provision of mass-produced, cheap literature which would help extend the reading public but itself demanded a literate work-force. Recently it has been demonstrated that whereas 52 per cent of traders and artisans dwelling in the East London suburbs of Stepney and Whitechapel in the period 1580–1639 were illiterate, only 24 per cent of the same groups living in the City of London itself were illiterate. This discrepancy even within the capital, where the rate of literacy was abnormally high, has been attributed to the fact that the waterfront traders of the suburbs had less need of literacy than the men engaged in the printing and other skilled trades of the city. Over the country the proportion of workers involved in this type of trade must have been small but even in rural areas farmers and traders were coming to need at least the ability to read. The early seventeenth century saw a huge increase in the number of credit dealings, owing to a shortage of money in circulation, and this, coupled with an expansion in private dealing outside the market, meant that those engaging in internal trade had to be able to read the bipartite bonds which they signed or risk their money. Dealings in land made some degree of literacy desirable if fair play were to be ensured.

Men engaged in other types of work also required schooling to a greater or lesser degree. It is well known that early modern England was a litigious age. Crown, common law and ecclesiastical courts all saw a huge expansion of business. They required a commensurate increase of personnel at all levels to deal with this extra work. Notaries, apparitors, registrars, proctors, advocates as well as judges all required basic literacy and, in many cases, a grammar school education and some kind of higher education to equip them for their jobs. An expanding governmental bureaucracy also made demands upon the educational system.

Important also for the provision of both higher and secondary education during the period was the feeling that the clergy of the Church of England should be well educated—if possible, to degree level [13]. In common with the reformed churches of the Continent, English Protestants believed that the reformed ministry had to be well instructed if it were to be capable of instructing, caring for and disciplining the people. There were well over 9,000 livings in England and Wales. Each parish had to be served by at least one minister. In addition there were cathedral chapters, collegiate churches, hospitals, colleges and chapelries all served by men in orders. Clearly an attempt to provide just this section of the community with a formal education would make a considerable impact upon the educational picture in Britain [14 a & b].

The very nature of the education to be extended to men of the professional classes and to sons of the gentry destined for places in central government or local magistracy meant that formal and professional tuition was necessary. The humanist curriculum of the grammar schools where most of these boys were to be educated was based upon classical studies—obviously far in advance of anything the average father or master could offer. It was not even desirable that the apprentice priest or lawyer be encouraged to pick up the necessary skills from their elders because existing professional standards were so appalling. The humanist curriculum reflected the view of the Christian humanists that through education new men could be trained to serve a new society. As will be indicated, the grammar school was no less a vehicle of social engineering (conceptually) than schools specifically set up for the training of the poor in useful crafts.

*The provision of formal education*

Each and every one of these influences was reflected somewhere in the educational system. System, however, is perhaps the wrong word to use when looking at schooling during the period. Before discussing how widespread the provision of schooling was at this time, it is necessary to examine the types of schooling which were offered.

At this time, elementary, secondary and higher education were available and the traditional view of Tudor and Stuart education has been one of Petty (ABC) and Grammar (Latin) schools and of the two ancient universities, Oxford and Cambridge. This is far too simple a picture. Many schools had a mixed character. Although most of the endowed grammar schools professed to teach classical subjects to boys who were already both literate and versed in the rudiments of Latin grammar, most were forced to make provision for the tuition of small boys in Latin accidence before their entry to the grammar school proper. Shrewsbury school's statutes, for instance, stipulated that a fourth master should be appointed who would have sole charge of the 'Accidence School' for young beginners, which school should be kept in or near the grammar school. In 1609 Wolverhampton Grammar School had two masters and 69 pupils, 41 of the boys were divided into two forms and a petties' class under the control of the usher (under-master) while 28 boys formed the three top classes under the headmaster's tuition. The age distribution of the pupils is very significant. Only 9 boys were in the top class, that devoted to preparing boys for professional careers and the universities. Wolverhampton school, unlike that at Shrewsbury, drew its boys from the immediate locality and served the needs of the neighbourhood. For most of these pupils this need was for a preparation for apprenticeship—the acquisition of basic literacy and accounting, and probably little more. Only a small proportion of the boys continued their secondary education and yet fewer ever progressed to higher education. It is probable that in a town school of this type the petties' class provided instruction in basic literacy as well as in Latin accidence. Some larger schools, situated in more developed areas, such as St Paul's in London or Shrewsbury school, may have felt more able to restrict entry to the accidence school to boys already literate in the vernacular.

The endowed grammar schools, however, did not restrict their activities either to academic subjects or to the teaching of classical Latin and Greek. It is evident that for many boys the school set out to provide the skills they would need when training for their jobs. It is in such as Sir Gervase Sleigh's will that may be found the most significant traces of the non-classical, non-religious side of the curricula of the endowed schools [15]. His son, Hugh, was to learn reading, writing, arithmetic and accounting until he was 17, specifically to fit him to be apprenticed to a merchant. It must have been fairly unusual for a boy to pursue an almost entirely vernacular education to such an advanced age—one must conclude that Hugh would eventually become factor to a merchant, an occupation requiring rather more skill than most other non-professional occupations. Nevertheless, it is significant that Hugh was receiving this education at none other than Repton school, which was also responsible at the same time for the preparation of his elder brothers, Samuel and Gervase, in classical subjects prior to their further education at Gray's Inn and Cambridge respectively.

The academic curricula followed in grammar schools were not purely classical in intent or content. It is now generally accepted that the creed which dominated the schools may have been humanist but it was nevertheless Christian. St Paul's school, founded by Dean Colet, pursued a classical curriculum which placed due emphasis upon Latin grammar, composition and rhetoric, but the manuals prepared by Colet, Erasmus and Lily for the use of the scholars indicated that these skills were to be handmaids, enabling the boys to come to a full understanding of the content of classical culture. Moreover, a catechist was provided to instruct young catechumens in the basic principles of religion and, in the grammar forms, Latin epigrams and Erasmus's moral verses were employed to impart knowledge of moral precepts and desirable manners to the pupils. Shrewsbury school followed a traditional classical curriculum but felt itself very responsible for the Christian upbringing of its boys. Pupils were taken to Sunday and weekday church services; they were made to take notes on sermons and to answer questions relating to the text; they were catechised by a minister employed for the purpose; they read the Scriptures; they were boarded out during term time with Protestant families. The statutes of some schools laid great emphasis, more than purely formal, upon their religious function. In 1606 Wakefield school, a 'seminary for bringing up of Christian children' set the duty of the master to 'instruct and inform his scholars in the grounds of religion' above that of teaching them classical languages.

In some cases this emphasis upon Christian education reflected more than a general anxiety that Christian and specifically Protestant views and knowledge be perpetuated—it mirrored the fact that the schools were 'seminaries' in a more conventional sense. Until the late sixteenth century the highest form of education the average parochial priest or curate received was in the local grammar school—although, of course, large numbers of the higher clergy and of the non-resident parish clergy were university trained. When it became normal for the lower clergy to take university degrees, they still passed through the grammar schools and small private schools in droves. By far the largest number of boys staying on into the classical forms of the grammar schools were destined to become lawyers or clergymen, and many were themselves sons of men in holy orders. There seems little doubt that the curriculum of the schools was slanted towards their needs. Continental texts produced by Genevan Protestants replaced those of Erasmus and Vives, both Catholic although humanist, in many English schools. Where Greek and Hebrew were taught they were studied as Scriptural rather than as classical languages. Latin itself was essential for anyone hoping to attend university and receive orders.

The 'secondary' schools of England were not offering a classical education which bore little or no relevance to the lives of their students. Firstly, the curriculum was not exclusively classical. As has been shown, the curriculum was moulded to suit the needs of boys proceeding to higher education. Also French and German began to be taught in some established schools in the seventeenth century and commercial subjects and vernacular skills were an integral part of many school timetables. Contemporary thinkers were somewhat divided as to the place of modern languages in the schools. In 1654 John Webster expressed the opinion that knowledge of foreign languages betokened no intellectual stimulation; Sir William Petty felt that the learning of languages required maturity; John Dury actually recommended, in 1650, the establishment of schools specifically for language teaching. By and large it appears that language teaching held a more prominent position in private schools, particularly in the capital where there was constant demand for merchants, teachers, bureaucrats, lawyers and courtiers skilled in 'tongues', but school statutes rarely reflect the diversity in the grammar schools' timetable. They did provide a preparation for various types of career—commercial, professional, magisterial.

There was no conformity: a large endowed school in an area already rich in educational facilities, such as London, might well be more restricted in function than a smaller school in a provincial market town which had to serve the needs of all sections of the community. Because of this a neat division of Tudor and Stuart schools along class lines will not work—the grammar school often did cater for more boys entering the lower trades and crafts than for those entering the mercantile trades and professions. Two conclusions are permissible: grammar schools were fulfilling a largely urban function—although they drew many boys from rural areas, who tabled out (boarded) in the town during term in order to attend, most of these boys were seeking entry to urban life; the grammar schools may not have been restricted to what we would call middle-class entrants but their curriculum was certainly structured along class lines—boys entering trades and crafts followed completely different studies from those entering the professions, or those hoping to become merchants, and the length of the secondary course pursued by these different classes of pupil differed sharply. The minimum age of apprenticeship for various crafts and trades obviously determined these differences to some extent. The historian's knowledge of the structural arrangement of the grammar schools is restricted, largely because today's system of streaming into classes according to age and ability was comparatively unknown. Many so-called 'classes' were taught in one room; the groups often were based upon the stage reached in the classical curriculum but the method of teaching the whole class simultaneously was unknown and work was individually pursued by the pupils. Because of this, it was quite possible for one 'class' to contain boys studying different subjects or different aspects of the same subject.

A view of Tudor and Stuart elementary and secondary education which concentrated exclusively upon the grammar schools would be unrepresentative. On the one hand there was a significant body of more ephemeral but no less important institutions which included what were later to be called Dame or ABC schools; local schools maintained by town corporations, local subscription, parental fees or some combination of these means; schools which depended for their existence upon the enterprise and presence of an itinerant schoolmaster or village priest or curate; or groups of boys receiving tuition from a privately-hired tutor [16]. If the endowed schools conformed to no pattern, the unendowed did so even less. In trying to determine their number, their character or their importance in the life of the country, the historian meets nothing but obstacles. These schools normally had no statutes or ordinances. They left no records of their own. More often than not they had no permanent school buildings (although many of those supported by local authorities were properly established in distinct buildings). Often they were in existence for a few years only.

Theoretically, the Church of England controlled the provision of education in England and Wales. Schoolmasters were compelled by law to obtain ecclesiastical licences to teach. Schools were subject to inspection by church authorities. In fact, however, it was a simple matter to evade, intentionally or by accident, the arm of authority and, because licences were relatively expensive, many schoolmasters did so. Basically the church officials were interested in the larger schools, because they involved the greatest number of boys, were situated in the densest areas of population, and were concerned with the education of the socially significant classes—future clergy, lawyers, doctors and gentry. Spasmodic attempts, motivated by central instructions or financial need, were made to check up on licensing and, because of this, there exist lists of unlicensed schoolmasters practising in the dioceses at various times which can be used alongside licensing books to provide information regarding the location of schools [17]. Only very rarely, however, do ecclesiastical records provide any information about the curricula of such schools or the community response, enthusiastic or apathetic, to them.

*The distribution of schools*

The schools of England and Wales conformed to no pattern and were controlled by many different bodies. One would expect, therefore, a very uneven distribution of formal educational facilities throughout the country. Scholars have done relatively little work on the geographical spread of schools in the early modern period but enough has been accomplished to permit the historian to attempt a very few generalisations.

Evidence for provincial areas is of interest. The diocese of Coventry and Lichfield (Derbyshire, part of Shropshire, Staffordshire, and part of Warwickshire) contained 388 parishes with their chapels. Research shows that at least 93 of these parishes had a continuing tradition of educational provision at some level and, probably, a proper establishment. Predictably the schools followed the population and the trade routes. Stafford archdeaconry, for example, had 18 market towns and 15 of these had a school by the early seventeenth century; one more probably had a grammar school by the outbreak of civil war; the remaining two had a schoolmaster for some part of the time at least. There were other fairly large parishes, without markets, which had schools in Staffordshire. Some qualifications are necessary. Market towns were not always centres of large population (Cheadle, Staffs; Burton, Staffs; Southam, War.; and Rugby, War. were all market towns but were small even by contemporary standards) but they normally possessed a school because they had a trading hinterland which would make use of the town's social and educational facilities. Some small parishes which were not market towns did support schools but they were in the minority. Several larger parishes, also not market towns, did not have permanent schools but a glance at a map shows why. The parishes concerned (Sedgeley, Leigh, Yoxall, Westbromwich, Stowe and Cheswardine) were situated very near towns with schools. Sedgeley and Westbromwich, for example, were exceedingly close to grammar schools in Walsall, Wednesbury and Great Bloxwich; Stowe was near to Colwich and Stafford. Boys might well have to table out in the town if the schools were as much as ten miles away from the village, but it remains true that those of the requisite economic status normally had access to elementary schooling within walking distance from home and to secondary schooling if they could afford to board out during at least the winter months. Moreover, so much of the actual population lived in the very towns which had the schools that the geographical/population spread of educational opportunities was really exceptionally good. These findings are substantiated by work completed and in progress on other areas of England, including Leicestershire and the Home Counties. Moreover, the work of Mr P. Locatelli on the diocese of Auxerre in France in the seventeenth century has indicated the strong connection between the growth of schools and the existence of market towns and trading routes.

Recent work on Cambridgeshire by Margaret Spufford has shown that the availability of schooling varied even within a county. North of Cambridge, the villages on the fen edge both to the west and east were well provided with opportunities for continuous schooling in the late sixteenth and early seventeenth centuries, and to the south of Cambridge the same situation prevailed. There were, however, two exceptions: a line of villages running from Balsham to Borough Green, and villages west of Cambridge on the clay plateau out to Bourn, were not provided with permanent established schools although many employed a schoolmaster at various points in time. It seems that this corresponds with the economic development of the county: the fen and valley areas were expanding whereas the boulder clay settlements to the west had hit hard times. Work on three specific villages indicated that in general it was the prosperous yeomen of these rural communities who demanded education and made most use of the facilities. The school in the prosperous fen village of Willingham, for instance, was endowed by public subscription in 1593; this support came mostly from half-yardlanders in the community who could afford to donate an amount equivalent to two years' rent. They endowed the school because they wanted their children to be literate. On the whole, literacy and prosperity were very closely related.

Locatelli, looking at schooling in a French diocese, indicated that the relationship between schooling and prosperity was bound to be high. In 1695 the bishop had enjoined that every parish set up two schools, one for boys and one for girls; that all should attend until 14; and that a schoolmaster be appointed. The responses to these orders were diverse. Wooded areas provided fewest schools and those which were set up were situated in towns; purely agricultural communities were rather more enthusiastic but once again the schools clustered in market areas; the most prosperous region of the diocese responded well, providing schools in over half its parishes despite the absence of towns. In many cases the poor response seems to have been due to lack of funds. Teachers were dependent for their meagre salaries upon fees paid by the parents according to a set scale. Many parents resisted because they wished their children to work—by sending them to school they lost their children's labour and, in addition, actually had to pay for the privilege.

Thus it is clear that the expansion of educational facilities and the rate of school attendance was dependent upon the existence of surplus income which both obviated the need for the child's labour and/or income from that labour, and also enabled the parent to pay necessary fees. Even where there was a school, often with an apparently large enrolment, attendance was often seasonal, as children in rural areas would still be expected to help with the harvesting. In England many of the endowed grammar schools were termed 'free' but this normally meant that children of 'freemen' of the borough or, occasionally, of all town inhabitants were excused tuition fees. Children coming in from rural areas had to pay for tuition and, often, board and lodging. All were required to pay entry fees, extraordinary payments, and to buy books and equipment. The very expansion of schooling is an indication of the prosperity of a society and it is most important to establish which sections of the community were able to use both schools and universities. Although it is true that many parents and children, then as today, were willing to make sacrifices to pay for educational opportunity because they thought it desirable, either in itself or as a long-term investment, such families had to be able to subsist. There were, of course, exhibitions and scholarships to maintain some boys at school and university but relatively few of the flood of youths who attended Oxford and Cambridge in the 1620s, for example, must have had all their expenses covered in this way.

### *The 'third University' of England*

Although England and Wales were still predominantly agricultural and although the economy was still largely a subsistence economy, there were significant exceptions to the rule. The growth of London was rapid and enormous—in population it far outstripped the other significant cities of the kingdom. All, however, owed their expansion primarily to their importance as coastal or internal ports and market centres. As a general rule the fortunes of the ports fluctuated according to the state of their export trade. London, of course, had additional advantages—it had become the centre of government, especially now that the court was less peripatetic than in earlier centuries. The case of London provides an excellent, indeed unparalleled, example of the relationship between the establishment of institutions of formal education and urban growth and prosperity. The city had a trade/commercial base and function; people engaged in such occupations needed to be literate. This particularly applied to overseas merchants and their factors, ambassadors and diplomats, Customs officials, civil servants, and craftsmen engaged in the printing industry or in the making of watches, clocks, arms, and navigational instruments. Society in London was of a far more complex structure than elsewhere in England. More men were engaged in such occupations which demanded at least some degree of literacy and so the establishment of many different types of school was economically viable. Children were less likely to attend irregularly.

It is interesting to note that school provision in the capital catered for just these needs. London has been called the 'third University' but it was certainly no ivory tower from whose dreamlike existence scholars looked out on to the real world. Private schools designed to fit boys for a life in commerce grew up all over London. John Mellis, for instance, taught reading, writing, drawing and arithmetic in Southwark in the 1590s and one Humphrey Baker established a boarding-school conveniently situated near the Royal Exchange. The emphasis was upon modern subjects taught in the vernacular and not in Latin. In 1596 Gresham College was established—lectures were delivered in English on the seven liberal arts but it should be noted that lectures were given not only on pure astronomy but on its application and on geography and navigation. Its scientific emphasis indirectly led to the foundation of the Royal Society. Gresham College was not alone in providing instruction in useful subjects: scientific lectures were given at Leadenhall chapel; there was a cosmography lecture at Blackfriars; Deptford 'college' taught hydrography and navigational studies; there was increasing provision for instruction in contemporary languages, including French, German, Persian, Turkish, Russian and other Slavonic languages useful in commerce and diplomacy. The development of modern language teaching echoes the situation in early sixteenth-century Antwerp, where the demands of international trade led to the establishment of language schools. In London several private establishments imparted warlike skills, such as the use of arms and fencing. Other academies were set up to prepare youth, male and female, for the fashionable society which was now emerging. There were painting, dancing and music schools, and finishing schools for girls, which latter particularly flourished under Charles I and the later

Stuarts. Professional education was not neglected. Common law was studied, if somewhat haphazardly, at the fashionable law clubs—the Inns of Court; attorneys and solicitors still obtained some instruction at the Inns of Chancery; civil lawyers gathered at Doctors' Commons. There was little real provision for the study of medicine, mainly because those who were really interested went to one of the great European centres—such as Padua— for instruction, but it is significant that during the seventeenth century the College of Physicians began to provide lectures in medicine.

Indeed the only one of the learned professions for which no formal provision was made in the capital appears to have been the Church. Doubtless this was because the universities were traditionally organised as seminaries and because, during this era of the new foundation and re-foundation of colleges on Protestant lines, the re-modelling of clerical education was relatively easy and much cheaper within the existing framework. Even here, however, it should be noted that the bishops of London were to the fore in providing in-service training and examination of the clergy and that attempts were made by individual men and parishes to provide religious education supplementary to that offered by incumbents through the media of parish lectures.

The ancient universities had driven out the disciplines of law and medicine to a great degree and were concentrating more than ever upon their clerical function. Chairs and college lectureships had been established in modern subjects but the emphasis of university education was not in these areas. A new emphasis upon the B.A. course, as opposed to the M.A. and other higher degree courses, meant that the universities were increasingly offering a general education in traditional, theoretical disciplines to future clerics and to gentle and noble youths seeking just such a general education. The position of the universities in provincial backwaters meant that they did not attract new types of educational foundation—it was far more logical that merchants and traders should establish their schools and academies in the centre of commerce, London, and that the clubs of the common lawyers should be located near the central law courts.

London was well provided also with traditional forms of school. The diocese of London had at least 149 grammar schools in the period 1627–85. 43 of these were in the city itself (a very small area) and there were many more in the immediately surrounding parishes. There is some indication that the grammar schools were on the decline in the later seventeenth century or, at least, that the study of Latin was losing ground. 27 of the city grammar schools disappeared in the later years of the century and many became English schools. In part, this was because fewer graduates were applying for licences and it was the custom of the ecclesiastical authorities to license only graduates to teach Latin but, in part, the decline may also be attributable to increasing use of the vernacular and a feeling that classical education did not offer the best training for adult life.

*Conclusion*

No brief essay can do justice to the diversity of English educational facilities in the early modern period nor to the very many ways in which these institutions served, and were seen to serve, the demands of both economy and society. Some general conclusions are called for, however, to facilitate future study and thought along these lines. Firstly, it has been shown that the system of apprenticeship fulfilled some of the needs of a society in which some of the young, at least, entered occupations foreign to their home environment, but that it was an economically wasteful method of training future craftsmen and tradesmen. It has also been shown that the system promoted both occupational and geographical mobility but confirmed class divisions within society. Secondly, the period studied saw a demand for formal schooling which had its roots in several factors—the religiously-motivated call for mass literacy; the Puritan view that education would enable the child to find his God-given vocation; the Protestant view that the school environment must be consciously employed by the Godly to counteract the evil influences of family and home; the undoubted fact that more and more jobs required basic literacy, a grammar school education or higher education. Thirdly, the spread of educational facilities has been described—demonstrating that different schools served different needs in the community and that the distribution of schools was closely related to the distribution of prosperous, urban societies. Finally, the manner in which the peculiar economic structure of the capital called into existence equally atypical educational facilities has been emphasised.

# 4

# The Demand for Capital in Pre-Industrial England

During the first half of the twentieth century many English and American historians assumed that the sixteenth and seventeenth centuries in England saw the beginnings of capitalist society. Professor R. H. Tawney, following the thesis of the German sociologist, Max Weber, thought that the period witnessed the 'triumph of the economic virtues' and believed that tendencies within Puritanism made it the 'potent ally of the movement against the control of economic relations in the name either of social morality or of the public interest' which was to come into its own in post-Civil-War England. Sanctification of the profit-making motive was what he described. The American, J. U. Nef, postulated that the England of the era 1540–1640 witnessed both an industrial and a technological revolution, previously ignored by historians concentrating on the industrial advances of the late eighteenth and the nineteenth centuries, which created demands for capital investment (of both the fixed and circulating nature) and created a capitalist relationship between employer and labour-force more typical of the modern than of the medieval traditionalist society.

Such assumptions as these have been tested both directly and indirectly by historians since they were broached in the 1920s and 30s. The facts have been released from the strait-jacket of Marxist thought. It is undoubtedly true that both Tawney and Nef were describing accurately and with insight one part of the picture, but it was only a very small part. No historian today would wish to detract from the very real value of their researches and ideas. Nevertheless it is important to note that in the sixteenth and seventeenth centuries in rural areas, anything between 50 and 80 per cent of the labour-force were still *fully* occupied by agriculture and, even in so-called 'industrialised' rural areas, a great proportion of the remainder were involved only partially in industrial production. Professor Nef distorted our view of the industrial sector also by laying emphasis upon the development and organisation of the coal and iron industries. Recent calculations suggest that, in all, coal-mining throughout England in the *late* seventeenth century (when demand for the product was much increased) accounted for a labour-force of between 12,000 and 15,000 men: this number represented but a quarter of those employed as merchant seamen and a tenth of those employed in tanning and associated leather manufactures. Yet the bulk of the 'industrial' man-power in seventeenth-century England was not employed in what we would term high 'manufacture' at all. Although the production of wool and woollen cloth has been given undue prominence by the detailed attentions of historians (and was certainly of colossal importance in England's export trade) it dominated the occupational structure of only a very few rural areas and towns in England (for example, Worcester, Coventry and Norwich). In fact, the production and preparation of food and drink had a far more universal impact upon occupational structure. Innkeepers (who normally brewed their own perishable light beers and ales), brewers, maltsters and butchers were the most prevalent.

In this chapter we shall be trying to assess the sort of demand that there was for capital investment and the extent of existing outlets for capital in early modern England. In doing this we shall be bound to emphasise those areas which did demand capital outlay—for instance, the production of iron or coal—and describe the organisation and evolvement of such industries, but we must continually remind ourselves that these were *relatively* small and insignificant sectors of the economy.

### *Coal-mining* [18]

There was certainly some demand for capital investment in industrial enterprise. This took two basic forms: fixed investment in plant; and circulating investment in the form of stock, raw materials and so forth, normally described as working capital. The level of fixed capital investment, even in an industry as relatively reliant on technology and machinery as mining, varied with the size of the venture. A coal-mine functioning at Sheffield between July 1579 and December 1582 was on a very small scale, employing no more than four or five face workers and a few men who drained the mines. The mine 'appears to have been totally unmechanised'. The miners used picks and wooden shovels by the light of candles. The coal once hewn was dragged in baskets to the shaft, where it was hauled to the surface by a rope and pulley-wheel. The mine itself was drained in the most primitive manner—by men in relay teams drawing water in buckets. The miners themselves were the only permanent employees of the mine; the 'drainers' were, for the most part, casual workers, although on occasion the miners themselves were employed in this work. The 'drainers' earned between threepence and sixpence a day or eightpence to tenpence for a day and night. The miners (two to four pickmen, a barrower, a bankman, and occasionally a helper) were paid at piece rates; according to the ideal rate of productivity the pickmen and barrower would earn sixpence a day and the bankman ninepence but in fact earnings normally fell below this rate. The bankman had to pay the helper out of his own wage. Yearly earnings amounted to perhaps £6 1s. 10d. for pickmen and barrower and £9 2s. 10d. for the bankman. Overheads also included a retainer fee of £1 6s. 8d. per annum for the services of the blacksmith; payments of between sixpence and eightpence a day to carpenters employed in lining the shafts and fitting 'punches' in the pits; a fee of sixpence a day to the thatcher who worked on the small hut placed at the top of a shaft; and a rate of fourpence a load to the cutters and carriers of the punch-wood. The few raw materials demanded little outlay. Wood, the main item, was provided free from the Earl of Shrewsbury's woods. It could not be said that he would have got a higher return had he sold the wood because this type of wood (not shipping timber) was in plentiful supply and brought low prices, except when there were local shortages. Candles cost about £5 a year. Pit-ropes cost about £1 or a little more each year. Mining tools were very cheap—a miner's shovel cost as little as a penny or twopence—and the steel required for the blacksmith to make the pit-head gear never cost more than a shilling per year. Nails cost but a few pence and strikes to light the candles perhaps eightpence per annum.

No estimate of profits and overheads can be deduced from the accounts because these normally deducted the overheads in terms of candles and wages from the coal profits item. Professor Lawrence Stone does suggest, however, that the balance sheet of January 1580 to January 1581 might well show a profit of £55 16s. 9½d. on coal production and a holding of £117 19s. 11½d. Small-scale enterprises of this type do not tell the whole story. Huntingdon-Beaumont is reputed to have invested between £6,000 and £7,000 developing collieries in the north-east of England during the early seventeenth century. Yet even by the end of the seventeenth century, only 30 or 40 collieries were providing employment for as many as 30 or 40 permanent workers apiece and it has been said that, for every pit sunk deep and requiring reasonably heavy outlay in sophisticated boring and drainage equipment, there were a dozen shallow shafts perfectly capable of being worked and drained by primitive methods and organised by co-operation of independent miners.

### *Iron*

The production of iron ore provides more striking evidence of the need for both fixed and working capital in industrial enterprise. It is estimated that during the sixteenth century it was possible to erect a furnace and forge with the necessary working equipment and buildings for between £100 and £200; by the seventeenth century the cost had risen to between £400 and £500. On occasion costs were much higher. In 1541 a furnace and forge were built near Robertsbridge Abbey, Sussex. By December 1542 the unusually high sum of £253 had been spent on construction. Of £131 9s. 11½d. spent on the construction of water-courses, at least £93 9s. 6½d. had been spent on the diversion of a stream to serve the forge site. In 1543 a second furnace was built at Panningridge nearby. For a time the two were worked simultaneously but then the one at Robertsbridge ceased operation until 1576. The new furnace cost £65 16s. 9d., plus a rental of £21 per annum for the site and transport costs which were to add 5 per cent to the cost of a ton of pig-iron in 1546. Yet, as D. W. Crossley's work indicates, even after all these overheads, the profit margin at Panningridge in the late 1540s seems to have been 53 per cent. An outstanding example of capital investment in ironworks has been brought to light by Professor Stone in his essay on the activities of the Manners, Earls of Rutland. The 1st Earl set out to modernise the medieval works at Rievaulx in 1540 when he installed a water-powered hammer. In the mid-1570s the 3rd Earl erected the first blast furnace in the north of England, extended the casting floor, built a new forge, and hired a Staffordshire refiner's services. Until the Civil War the works was the most up-to-date in the north of England and the seventeenth century witnessed several innovations including a new furnace at the cost of £104, the first English use of forge slag, and the first instance of arching over the furnace apertures. These technological innovations reaped considerable dividends in terms of productivity: rising costs were more than cancelled out by rising prices paid for the iron. By the 1620s a labour-force of some 80 men was required to work the plant but most work was done at piece-rates by casual workers who could be laid off when their services were not required. It appears that for most of the year approximately 30 woodcutters, 8 general labourers, 12 miners for ore, 9 carriers of ore and charcoal, 6 carriers of wood and 4 to 6 colliers were employed and there was an additional permanent staff of clerk of the works, storekeeper, overseer, founder, chafery man, 3 finers and a woodward, plus the auditor.

The owners of ironworks were heavily dependent upon raw materials, especially wood. It is notable, therefore, that there was a marked attempt to achieve vertical integration in the metallurgical industry. The Earls of Rutland attempted to fuel their works from the estate woods. Once cut, a wood would not yet be ready for felling for a further fifteen years; the prudent 1st Earl organised his supplies so that twenty separate areas were cropped in sequence, thus maintaining a steady supply. When productivity of iron expanded particularly quickly in the early seventeenth century in a concerted attempt to capture the London market, it became clear that the demand for wood could not be met from the estate alone—some 3,000 to 4,500 acres of woodland were required to maintain the necessary supply of fuel and this was more than the Earl possessed. Approximately one-third of the raw material had to be purchased. The Panningridge works remained virtually self-contained until well into the 1550s. By the 1560s, however, it seems that much of the necessary woodland had been permanently cleared for agriculture and wood for charcoal had to be purchased. It is possible that this was due to the obsolescence of the ironworks by this date. Certainly the works hit hard times in the 1560s with difficulties in the supply of ore itself, rising transport charges and increasing wages, and there was perhaps a reduced demand for iron in the 1560s.

It could be said, therefore, that although the capital necessary for equipment, wages, raw material and day-to-day maintenance in the metallurgical industries was relatively large compared with many industries, it happened that iron-smelting on a large scale was often sponsored by large landowners who possessed not only the mineral resources themselves but also the woods which provided the basic raw material and the water necessary both for power and transport. The need for outside investment was minimised. Once the initial costs of providing dam, millpond, stream, buildings and new equipment had been overcome, the Manners Earls of Rutland found that by far the heaviest running expense was on wages. Prior to 1614 annual overheads were approximately only £500; these rose to £1,200–£1,500 in the 1620s due to the need to purchase wood; after a further rise they fell again in the 1630s to around £1,500. The efficiency of the industry and the effectiveness of the Earls' marketing ensured profits of between £1,000 and £1,500 per annum between 1601 and 1640.

The iron industry was certainly expanding in the sixteenth and seventeenth centuries. Initially most blast-furnaces were situated in the Sussex Weald, Kent and Surrey: in 1574 51 of the 58 blast-furnaces were in the Weald. Costs of wood and labour rose in the area towards the end of the century and the Weald gave way in some measure to other areas—the Forest of Dean, South Wales, Yorkshire and the west Midlands—so that by 1653, when the number of furnaces in blast in the country as a whole had risen to 70, only 36 of these were in the Weald. More significant perhaps is the fact that iron-mining and smelting can only have provided employment for a few thousand men in the country. The preparation of leather and allied crafts provided work for a far greater proportion of the population and a study of its organisation is valuable as an indication of capital demand.

### *Leather*

The leather industry can be divided into two main sections—tanning or the heavy branch of the craft, and the light leather crafts. Employees in the latter had country-wide distribution as they included the shoemakers but, in general, the leather industry was concentrated upon urban areas. In some places, where there was ready availability of hides, water and other raw materials, the industry dominated the town's occupational structure—as in Leicester and Northampton. By the early eighteenth century the industry seems to have provided work for some 150,000 persons in England and Wales. The reason for the urban concentration of the industry—particularly of tanning—is of importance: the butchers who provided large quantities of meat for the town population also provided hides for preparation. It is not surprising that the industry was most lively in London itself (where the greatest quantity of meat was consumed) nor that a town like Leicester with 27 butchers should find itself a centre for the industry. Once again this is a striking example of the way in which overheads were kept low by the clustering of industry near the source of raw materials.

The leather crafts could be conducted with very small amounts of *fixed* capital. In the late sixteenth century a fully equipped tannery might be rented for £6 or less. A tanner, as opposed to a light leather worker, however, had need for considerable *working* capital. Tanning, as opposed to the dressing of light sheep, goat or calf skins, was a slow process and there was a need to space out the number of hides at different stages of the manufacturing routine so that there was always sufficient supply of finished hides for distribution and sale. Tanners were accustomed to have large stocks of hides for this reason. If tanners had high overheads in this respect they were able to execute economies of scale—they were more labour efficient than the light leather workers and craftsmen, whose organisation depended on the putting-out system. When a light leather worker wished to increase production he had to employ more labour; when the tanner wished to increase production he could normally do so by processing more hides with the same amount of labour. Inventories can provide a useful glimpse into the difference in scale between the working and fixed capital investment of tanners and light leather workers—for example, one Thomas Clerke, tanner of Huntingdonshire, was able to process £125 worth of leather in equipment valued at 18 shillings; a Boston shoemaker in 1636, on the other hand, while he had equipment appraised at 10 shillings, held stocks of completed shoes and leather worth just over £8. The fact that the cobbler worked quickly and catered for a personal and immediate market meant that he had far less need for working capital than the tanner, who for technical reasons had to hold large quantities of leather and, moreover, was seeking to reach a larger and more generalised market.

### *Cloth*

Historians have laid great emphasis upon the importance of the cloth industry in early modern England. One might think that the growth in cloth exports over the period was a reflection of increased efficiency and technical expertise within the industry. There is little indication that this was so. In order to escape the restrictive measures of the town guilds, after 1500 it became increasingly common for merchant-clothiers to buy up wool and put it out to rural workers for processing [19]. The fixed capital investment of the merchant was small—the necessary equipment was either owned or rented by the independent clothworkers. The merchant was disadvantaged to some extent. He had increased costs of distribution; difficulties of supervision of the product; and risks arising from pilfering and fraud on the part of his employees. Nevertheless, the savings in terms of equipment and the cheapness of the under-employed manpower of the countryside compensated him for this. The putting-out system also facilitated division of labour and cheap specialisation on particular types of cloth for specific markets, because large numbers of men were employed, and no heavy outlay was required for either factories or equipment. Until the introduction of the Dutch loom in the 1660s and the inventions of Kay and Paul in the 1730s, technical innovation was almost unknown in the industry and there was little stimulus towards the development of machinery or improved techniques as long as labour remained cheap. Increased demand for manufactured goods and rising wages in the late seventeenth and eighteenth centuries turned the attentions of manufacturers towards other ways of lowering costs of production and of increasing industrial output but, until technical problems were surmounted, the intensification of the putting-out system was the only viable, although increasingly uneconomic, method of organisation. The system had become typical of the clothing trades and the metallurgical crafts as well as the textile industry. Glove and stocking making, knitting, and leather work were also organised along these lines.

The putting-out system of industrial organisation reduced both the fixed and working capital investment of the merchant-industrialist but it has been noted that it created that division between management and worker which was to become typical of industrialised, capitalist society. It also served to weaken the power of the various trade and craft guilds which were town based—protection of both worker and consumer was reduced considerably.

The seventeenth century was certainly notable for the growing diversification of industrial enterprise within England. Imported sugar, tobacco and coffee stimulated processing industries in the port towns. Foreign immigrants, such as the Flemings and Walloons in the 1560s and the Huguenots in the 1680s, promoted the paper-making industry; introduced the manufacture of worsteds; improved brewing techniques; introduced a number of luxury industries; and gave rise to an expansion of the silk industry. Shipbuilding and associated crafts were important in many of the ports and shipbuilding an important employer of labour. Alum and salt works, iron-mining and smelting, copper-working and coal-mining were all expanding; while the traditional industries of woollen cloth, leather goods, and clothing continued to expand and adapt to the demands of new markets—but large-scale industrial ventures were very much the exception. Most industries were organised on small, simple lines. The greatest employers of labour were the putting-out industries. As has been shown, the capital overheads of these industries were low. There was no industrial revolution requiring large funds of capital.

### *Attempts to encourage capitalist investment*

The seventeenth century did witness considerable attempts to restructure industrial organisation in order to replace the failing medieval guild system and to attract capital investment. There was a need to make industrial investment attractive to the wealthy and also to reconcile the new investing/non-working class's interests with those of the existing producers. Initially investment was attracted by guaranteeing a market for a specific product—this was done by the granting of a patent of monopoly. Attempts to reconcile the interests of the two conflicting groups consisted mainly in the formation of chartered companies, designed to bring about investor/manufacturer co-operation in the exploitation of the consumer. All such attempts failed, some rapidly and dramatically like those in the soap, salt and starch industries—'where production was already in the hands of capitalists, opposition to the new regime was immediate and bitter'—some more slowly. The chartered companies are of importance, however, for they were an attempt to revitalise and modify the old guild system to meet the new circumstances. They strove to extend their jurisdiction outside the town and cover a wide area—the soap and starch companies, for instance, had national jurisdiction. The guild system had been urban because most manufacturing enterprise had been town-based, and for a restricted local market; now that industry was spreading into the countryside and now that markets were becoming much more extensive, there was a real need to reorganise the guilds on 'a territorial basis more in accord with economic realities'. This was particularly so, in the provinces, with relation to the textile industry. The new charters, however, offered few advantages to the producers—there was no guaranteed market by monopoly, only powers of inspection, and it was these very restrictive powers of the guilds which had first driven the manufacturers into the countryside.

Of yet more importance was an increasing feeling that industry needed not only regulation but fostering, encouragement, creation. In part, this arose out of a fear of unemployment and its social consequences and a desire to find work for the poor. The instruments chosen to encourage industrial development were the traditional ones—the guild, and the chartered company. As Professor F. J. Fisher has said, 'The difficulty was to persuade the investor to widen his interests, and to enter fields which offered neither the relative security of the patent nor the possibilities of immense wealth which imagination associated with coal', yet it was necessary to develop the textile industries and England's herring fisheries. The government had few weapons at its command which could attract capital into the herring industry—regulatory powers, taxes, tariffs and laws would repel rather than attract investment and a system of bounties was impracticable. A chartered company, on the other hand, might well be viable if it were given sufficient powers and privileges.

Projects for creative companies under the Stuarts fall under two broad categories—the monopolistic corporations (for example, salt and soap); and the regional joint-stock associations which aimed at mobilising the surplus moneys of gentry and merchants for industrial purposes and which were to be under some sort of public control. Unlike the chartered companies already mentioned, county joint-stock associations were designed not only to regulate but to establish industries. They were conceived as part of a national, integrated project, having a high degree of public control which, in some cases, amounted to 'direct public trading'. Professor Fisher sees them as 'revealing Stuart mercantilism in its most ambitious form, anticipating some of the most grandiose ideas of Colbert, and representing the nearest approach to national planning and state capitalism ever made in England'. The pioneer of the idea appears to have been Robert Hitchcock who advocated in 1581 the establishment of eight fishing associations centred on certain ports and financed by £10,000 each by the neighbouring rich. This plan formed the basis of the Fishery Society which actually appeared in 1632. The scheme failed because it did nothing to attract capital investment: no provision was made for extensive markets, guarantees against defrauding, or reduction of costs to enable the English to undercut Dutch prices. The project to develop the textile industries collapsed also. It began with the initiative of the Earl of Salisbury in 1608 in setting up textile manufacture in Hatfield, which became significant when an attempt was made to extend it to the whole of Hertfordshire. In 1616 a chartered company was formed of Bacon, Salisbury and twenty-seven of the leading Hertfordshire gentry to produce cloths not made elsewhere in England and sell them in unrestricted markets. The greatest defect of the scheme lay in the provision for recruiting capital— subscription was voluntary and the feeling that it would be some time before industry relying on unskilled labour could make a profit, let alone a guaranteed one, made investors reluctant. The plan failed. A second attempt was made to develop the industry during the slump of the 1620s—Salisbury's agent, Morrell, agitated for companies and in 1625 drafts were prepared for seven joint-stock companies based on county units: James I's death held up their passage [20]. Under Charles I the scheme was extended to some thirty-two counties but pressure of foreign affairs meant that the project was checked, this time never to be resurrected.

One may think that projects which either collapsed in practice or never left the drawing-board stage are not worth the historian's attention, but there is every reason to consider these attempts to expand industrial enterprise and to attract investment. Firstly, the economic climate of the time was very much in favour of state intervention in economic matters and the chartered company itself was considered an excellent means of control, yet the projects still failed. Secondly, the projects failed because the guild system was too inflexible to accommodate the new economic realities—they were not suited to the nascent competitive, capitalist spirit.

When all this has been said and it has been suggested that the amount of capital required by and achieved by industry was fairly low, it must be stressed that the seventeenth century saw a *relative* increase in the amount of capital investment needed and, moreover, that it witnessed the strengthening of the capitalist sectors within industry. This development was common to western Europe (with the possible exception of Spain); capital was provided more and more by merchant organisers as opposed to independent workers or small capitalist producers. As we have observed with reference to the cloth industry, this had the effect of creating true capitalist relationships within industry. Control of production was in the hands of a non-working merchant capitalist whose concern was with selling the product, making substantial profits, and so forth, rather than with meeting the specifications laid down by a guild. The division between rich capitalist and poor wage-earner was becoming a reality, which it had never been in a society of skilled craftsmen financing their own efforts to satisfy a limited local market. When considering the relevance of seventeenth-century developments for the later industrial history of England and Wales, this factor alone is of more importance than the actual quantity of capital required by industrial ventures.

*Methods of organising and financing trade*

Having established that the demand for capital investment in industry was increasing rapidly when compared with earlier years, it is interesting to move on to the example of both foreign and internal trade. The growth of agricultural specialisations and regional markets had a definite impact upon the means of organising and financing internal trade. The traditional open market was under acute pressure during this period. Merchants and middlemen were traversing England in an attempt to buy up supplies to furnish the metropolis, the export market, densely populated urban districts and, in time of war, large armies, with consumables and manufactured products. Merchants engaged in this type of work invested large sums of working capital in order to hold sufficient supplies of livestock, produce, and so forth. Serious losses could be suffered when, for example, cattle died *en route* from market and, in any event, the middleman had to wait some time before he had a return on his investment. When national markets began to emerge for given products, an even greater need for working capital was felt. In an age of slow, poor communications, merchants required more and more funds. Professor Davis gives the example of the national markets within France for the cloth of Rheims and Beauvais, which involved merchants in investing huge amounts of money to ensure that at any given time many bales of cloth were in transit, because transport of a bale from Beauvais to Grenoble, for example, took several weeks. Such transactions inevitably involved the merchant in a certain risk for he had no guaranteed market and could only judge by past performance and speculation as to market conditions. The situation in England was less dramatic since distances were not so great; nevertheless, supplying the densely-populated areas and some of the towns did involve quite large-scale investment. Merchants attempted to cut their risks by utilising existing river and canal transport and by supporting local attempts to improve these facilities. Inland merchants also could expect expenses in connection with warehousing and with transport equipment (including barges, fodder and grazing for livestock). Increased demand for manufactured and luxury items at the end of the seventeenth century (especially in the towns) had its impact upon the financing and organisation of this branch of internal as well as foreign trade.

The question of the organisation and financing of foreign trade provides a far more dramatic example of change, however. Until the acquisition and exploitation of her distant colonies in the Americas, most English foreign trade was over comparatively short distances. For such trade merchants did, of course, need capital. They had to buy or hire ships. Although the market within Europe depended upon a system of credit—merchants normally expected to sell manufactured goods and receive payment before being required to pay their own debts—reserves of capital were needed in case sales were unusually slow. Nevertheless, short-distance international merchants had little need for large-scale capital to finance their transactions on a regular basis. Merchants trading over great distances undoubtedly did. Merchants trading with the colonies were themselves selling manufactured goods, as in Europe, but they were importing in exchange agricultural and forest products. A merchant would purchase perhaps an entire colonial crop to be transported when ready and would pay for it in goods—he had to wait for his payment, and he had to wait even longer for his return on the investment. Thus he needed working capital to pay for his own credit from manufacturers at home, and to tide him over until he managed to bring the foreign cargo to the home market. The international merchant had other requirements—ships of bigger tonnage and capacity to make long journeys economical; supercargoes to supervise the cargo *en route*; factors in foreign ports.

Of course, one must not exaggerate the importance of foreign trade in the economy. For much of the sixteenth century, foreign exports and imports were dominated by foreign merchants, especially those of the Hanseatic League. As late as the 1540s, whereas about 55 per cent of woollen exports were shipped by the English Merchant Adventurers Company, the remaining 45 per cent were dealt with by Hanse merchants and other aliens. It was not until 1598 that the Hanse merchants were expelled from the country. Contemporaries also tended to exaggerate the importance of foreign trade, because of its significance as an attractor of precious metals and a source of government revenue. Yet it is true that foreign trade was expanding rapidly, both in terms of exports, imports and re-exports. It was the development of this re-export trade which was most significant: England became, as Professor Charles Wilson has put it, the entrepôt of Europe. This affected the tobacco, sugar and textile trades most notably. For example, in 1700 England imported 38 million pounds of tobacco: 13 million pounds were consumed at home and the remainder re-exported to Europe. West Indian sugar imports amounted to over 370,000 hundredweights by 1700 (more than double the post-Restoration figure): two-thirds were consumed at home; one-third was re-exported to European markets. The volume of imported calicoes increased by 3½ times between 1600 and 1700 and two-thirds of the imports were re-exported. Newfoundland fishing ships sold their cod harvest in the Mediterranean and returned with Mediterranean goods. Export cargoes went to West Africa, slaves were purchased with the profit and the colony plantations stocked with this labour, and the ships then returned to England with cotton for home consumption and re-export. All this called for large ships capable of taking bulk cargoes. L. A. Harper suggests that total tonnage grew from 150,000 to 200,000 tons in 1660 to 340,000 tons by 1688: 60 per cent was busy in Europe; 35 per cent in the Atlantic; 5 per cent in the eastern seas. By 1700 perhaps 10 to 12 per cent of the non-agricultural population was involved in merchant shipping.

One might expect, therefore, a dramatic change in the merchant community and its wealth during the period 1500 to 1700 and an even greater alteration in the organisation and financing of international trade. In a study of sixteenth-century Exeter merchants, Professor W. G. Hoskins describes a community dedicated to short-distance foreign trade. As late as 1597/8 50 per cent of trade was coastal, but in foreign trade most ships were trading with Brittany and the salt ports of western France; the remaining trade was with Newfoundland, Middelburg, Danzig, Portugal and Madeira. This Exeter port was certainly not as venturesome, for example, as Plymouth at the same period. The end of the sixteenth century did see the beginning of wider commercial interests in Exeter with trade to the Baltic, Holland and Spain expanding. By the late seventeenth century the trade with Holland was the most important. Yet the sixteenth-century community was just as merchant dominated—one-twentieth of Exeter families were of merchant occupation. Very few were wealthy enough to own a ship or half a ship; the most common practice was temporary organisation in groups of a dozen or so to fill a ship with cargo.

The demand for large amounts of capital brought about by longer-distance trading and its accompanying need for fortifications, warehouses, large-scale armoured ships, huge stockholdings and ready credit was catered for by a means of organisation which could tap the resources of the non-merchant as well as the merchant community—the joint-stock company. The most notable of these were the East India Company (1601), The Royal African Company and the Hudson's Bay Company, which gradually usurped the role of the old regulated companies—Eastland, Levant, Merchant Adventurers—in which all investors were active. Initially, common stock was formed for a single voyage but was dispensed with when the venture was completed. After some time the common stock became permanent and shareholders could leave the company by selling shareholdings. Limited liability companies, legal in Holland, were illegal in England; to some extent this restricted the attractiveness of the joint-stock companies for outside investors. Nevertheless the East India Company attracted surplus capital from nobles, gentry, shopkeepers, and so on, and the African Company recruited the investments of many courtiers, including the Queen and the Queen Mother.

As pointed out by Professor Hoskins, it was common for merchants to form partnerships for the purposes of trade. By the seventeenth century even the interloping merchants traded individually or in partnership. Individual shipowning did occur but shipowning syndicates and the practice of renting cargo-space were more common in long-distance, high-risk trading.

### *Capital demand in agriculture*

But it was neither industry nor trade which occupied the energies of most Englishmen at this time—rather it was agriculture. How much capital demand was there in the agricultural sector? There is no doubt that at this time land itself was the most popular form of investment in itself but, leaving this aside for the moment, what can the historian establish concerning the amounts of capital required for farming enterprise? Obviously this depended initially upon the size of the venture if the land itself had to be bought or improved, but the matter can be subjected to a more sophisticated analysis than this.

Historians utilise manorial accounts, the personal accounts of prosperous yeomen and gentry, wills, inventories and various other types of documentation to shed some light on the matter [21]. Problems arising from the nature of the documentation occur immediately—the manorial accounts rarely draw a clear distinction between capital and income, make allowance for the depreciation of capital assets (such as the deterioration of necessary equipment), allocate overheads to distinct parts of the venture, or assess the worth of produce consumed by the home farm. The approach of the yeomen and gentry farmers was often more business-like but the accounts probably do not accurately represent the state of their affairs. More serious is the complete absence of any accounts for the multitudinous smallholdings.

The arable smallholder with a farm of less than 30 acres in extent could farm his land without hired labour and his greatest capital expense was for seed; even if he were using seed from last year's crop this had to be deducted from his profit. The smallholder also had to pay rent per acre (30 times 4 shillings). These two items accounted for perhaps two-thirds of the farmer's outgoings, reflecting the uneconomic use of both land and seed in the period. Manure perhaps cost £2 5s. for 30 acres of enclosed land; a farmer working common field land spent perhaps half as much. Feed had to be provided for the oxen. Agricultural equipment was both simple and cheap. A plough, for example, could be got in Staffordshire for 1s. 8d. in 1582; even in 1621 one could purchase a plough in Norfolk for 3 shillings. It seems highly unlikely that the small arable farmer in the seventeenth century spent more than £3 (or 4 per cent of his probable expenditure) on equipment. The very small capital outlay required to run an arable as opposed to a pastoral farm turned most small peasant cultivators towards tillage or mixed farming with a bias towards tillage. Moreover, the arable farmer at this level could expect in average years (that is when there was no severe harvest failure) a profit of between £14 and £15 which compared favourably with the sort of income earned by an agricultural labourer (circa £9 per annum) and enabled him to live a comfortable if insecure life.

Although the small farmer broke even after one bad harvest because of increased grain prices, a run of disastrous harvests could not fail to ruin him because they deprived him of seed and because he could not pay his rent [22]. There seems to have been a point when a farm was sufficiently extensive in acreage to override such difficulties—perhaps between 50 and 100 acres—and to reap dividends from a general crop failure. Even if the larger farmer were no more efficient than the peasant cultivator, he inevitably had a larger market surplus because his home-consumption capacity was not increased in proportion to the size of his farm.

The farmer of a larger arable enterprise undoubtedly often paid higher rents than the smallholder. He normally farmed land which had been enclosed or otherwise improved by the landlord. This higher initial expenditure, however, brought its own reward in terms of higher yield per acre. By the late sixteenth century such farmers were also probably spending more money on manuring the land. In one respect, however, the larger farmer spent less money on his farm than did the smallholder. The smallholder could rarely keep a plough and its team fully employed —unless he hired it out to neighbours, it was relatively expensive in terms of productivity; the larger landholder, often, could farm a far more extensive holding with identical equipment and only a slightly increased labour-force. Dr Eric Kerridge discovered that a ploughteam of three or four horses would be used to farm an area of 60 acres in Wiltshire while only seven horses and a gelding were required to farm the land of Paul Dewes which amounted to between 100 and 150 acres. Of course, when two ploughs or more were used the amount of labour had also to be increased—a really large farm might employ as many as twenty workers as against the one, two or three normal employees of the two-plough farm or the entire lack of outside labour of the one-plough smallholding. Wages certainly accounted for a much larger proportion of the overheads of the large arable farm, perhaps over 36 per cent of total costs.

The large arable farmer had to grow highly profitable crops or increase productivity (through increased yield and more intensive farming) if he were to make an adequate living from his high-rent land, worked by expensive labour. To effect either of these improvements involved some additional capital expenditure in itself but ensured the large farmer as high a profit margin (proportionately) as the smallholder who hired no labour.

Dr Peter Bowden has constructed a model of the overheads and profits of a sheep farm of 400 acres of good pasture and 100 acres of rich meadowland during the early seventeenth century. This farm supposedly supports 1,000 wethers, 1,143 ewes and 38 rams. The initial outlay on stock was £1,200. The major part of the farmer's running expenditure was incurred in the provision of pasture (£330 or 13.20 per cent) and feed (£135 4s. or 5.41 per cent) for cattle and oxen. There was also, however, considerable capital depreciation (deaths, cost of paying interest on the initial purchase, etc.) The sheep-farmer may not have needed to employ much labour but he did need oxen for haymaking and transport, wood for sheep-folds and the labour to erect them, transport facilities, and money to cover marketing (tolls, drivers, overnight accommodation and food for the same). Labour had to be furnished at certain times of the year also—at haymaking, at sheep-shearing and so on. Dr Bowden's farmer had a total expenditure of some £767 16s. 1d., on which he showed a profit of £113 17s. 2d.

Sheep-farming was for obvious reasons unattractive to the smallholder and also out of his reach. It required little labour and would not keep a smallholder fully occupied. The capital outlay required to achieve an annual income equivalent to the £14 to £15 achieved by the peasant cultivator was enormous: about 158 sheep (costing between £80 and £90) and 36 acres of good enclosed pasture would be needed to make this amount of profit. It is easy to see why it appealed to the wealthy who wished to engage in commercial agriculture for the profits it offered but did not wish to become farmers in any real sense. As Dr Bowden points out, cattle-grazing was often combined with sheep-farming: it too could be managed from a distance and was attractive to sheep-rearers because of the complementary feeding habits of the two animals—reducing waste and increasing profit. One branch of cattle farming—dairy-farming—did appeal to small farmers. It required more labour, little capital outlay on equipment, and served a local market—there was more room for the small producer within the field.

The capital outlay of one other sector of the agricultural population remains to be considered—the *rentier* landlord. During the sixteenth century there was strong population pressure upon available agricultural land and a consequent upward pressure on rents. The terms of leases and copyholds often meant that the landlord could not benefit from the upward movement of rents immediately. The creation of new holdings as the acreage under cultivation increased helped the landlord offset this disadvantage and, where possible, existing rents were brought up to an economic level. Few landlords were entirely dependent upon rentals for their income; most had some interest in commercial agriculture and sheep-farming proved particularly attractive to the large landowner. Timber holdings also provided a source of revenue, although difficulties of transporting large timber over great distances prevented the full exploitation of these resources.

Landlords had certain calls upon their income—chief amongst these was the need for estate management and repair. Landlords attempted to reduce these costs. Attempts were made to load some of the work of manorial administration on to the tenants in lieu of higher rents. Many of the lessees of Sir William Petre after 1550 were obliged to serve as manorial officials (bailiff, reeve, etc.) and annual surveys of the Petre lands were compiled on the basis of terriers drawn up by the Petre tenants. Some landlords simply let farms on their manors decay to save expenditure on repairs. Others chose to 'engross' or group small farms together to form more economical, large farms. Increasingly the tendency was to make tenants responsible for repairs on their holdings. The landlord customarily provided the wood necessary to keep fences in repair. Occasionally tenants were even expected to foot the bill for estate improvement, such as the clearage of land for cultivation and its enclosure. When the tenant left such an improved holding he was not assured of compensation.

When a landlord was unable to raise money-rents to the economic level he sometimes resorted to the levying of rents in kind to furnish his home farm with produce, and feed his own animal livestock. Monastic landlords often received a considerable proportion of their rents in kind and by the seventeenth century produce-rents were an important part of the receipts from ecclesiastical lands. When leases and copyhold tenures were renewed or granted the landlord was able to adjust the rental temporarily to reflect rising land values, and entry fines were used to cushion the landlord against the effects of long tenancies upon his returns.

The costs of land improvement to the landlord could be enormous although the increase in productivity would be compensatory. Often landowners considered it worthwhile to mortgage their estates to finance such improvement. Certainly landed property remained a secure investment for men who had made their fortunes in other spheres than agriculture—for example, merchants. This was partially for economic reasons and partially because landownership was undoubtedly status conferring. Landowners made considerable capital investment in land improvement and increased productivity; they used their wealth to raise their standard of living and further family interests, but most of all they used it to build increasingly magnificent private mansions on their estates and to finance town houses and seasons in the metropolis. Professor Hoskins established that at least half a dozen Exeter merchants founded landed families. Typically such an estate would consist of one or two manors and farms in perhaps six or seven parishes. When he examined descriptions of 20 merchant houses built between 1564 and 1609 (not necessarily manor houses) he found that only 6 had fewer than 10 rooms, 11 had between 10 and 15 rooms and 3 had over 15 rooms. The merchant community at Exeter was not particularly wealthy compared with that of London or Bristol and yet even here there was considerable emphasis upon estate creation, house building and luxury commodities.

The country houses of Elizabethan and Stuart England have received much attention from historians, not so the considerable investment in urban property which took place during the same period. The town house has been mentioned, but the moneyed classes also invested money in *rentier* property in the metropolis. Professor Stone has described the investment of the Cecil family in the acquisition and development of urban property in London. In the early years of the seventeenth century Cecil bought a parcel of land on the Strand in order to build the 'New

Exchange'. This was to house a stock exchange and estate agency, and rows of small shops on two floors to cater for a fashionable clientele. The building was completed in a short period of time, using an unusually large, expensive labour-force. Elaborate rules were drawn up in 1609 for the governing of trading. Leases were to be granted only to traders in clothes, books, fancy goods, perfume and other luxury personal items. Sanitation was provided. The leases were costly—11-year terms at an entry fine of £30 and a rent of £10 per annum—and difficult to dispose of: by autumn 1609 only 27 out of about 100 had been taken up. The manager, Thomas Wilson, diagnosed the trouble as being lack of housing for the shopkeepers, the lack of storage facilities and the fact that the exchange was in a non-residential area with few natural customers. He proposed in remedy an ambitious, £20,000 plan to demolish Durham House and erect 100 houses. The Earl of Salisbury was in no position to do this—he had already spent £10,760 on the erection of the exchange in addition to an outlay of £1,200 to Archbishop Toby Matthew for the lease of the land. Interest rates on the money of 10 per cent per annum and annual maintenance costs meant that the Cecil family required an annual income of £1,200 a year if they were to have a reasonable return on their investment and this figure was only met between 1611 and 1617 when the project was being managed by a merchant syndicate of Customs farmers who paid Cecil £1,000 a year for the privilege. During the 1620s the scheme ran into serious financial difficulty and in 1623 Cecil was negotiating sale of the upper floor to Lady Hatton for £6,000. The project collapsed and the shops remained empty. By 1627 drastic re-thinking was necessary: the upper-floor shops were converted into flats. By the 1630s there was another economic reversal and the shops actually began to prosper. In 1638 Salisbury was tempted by this to buy back the leases of the flats and reconvert them into shops. His resolve was reinforced by a Privy Council order to clear the flats of tenants because of overcrowding in central London. The total cost to Salisbury was £1,030 on structural items. Although the Civil War led to a reduction in receipts, the exchange was booming by the early 1660s and the twenty years following saw the height of its prosperity. The Cecils handled the project shrewdly, responding to changing economic pressures and understanding the relationship of the prosperity of their own urban venture to the social and economic standing of the district of the West End in which it was situated. As a result, says Professor Stone, the 'proportion of the gross family income derived from urban housing rose fairly steadily from about 10 per cent before the Civil War to 37 per cent in 1720'.

Cecil's personal capital investment in the New Exchange plan was very considerable. His involvement in two other projects for urban development was less direct. The St Martin's Lane area was developed in the early seventeenth century as a residential area. In the 1620s the social standing of the land began to rise and the 2nd Earl of Salisbury attempted to reinforce this trend by inserting in leases the obligation of the tenant to build in brick to the tune of between £50 and £400. In 1632–4 the Earl combined with other eminent landlords in the area (Bedford, Suffolk and Leicester) to improve the property further by providing piped water and a sewer. He was personally involved to the extent of £525. The return on this considerable investment was slow, not becoming evident until the 1650s. Further residential improvement was undertaken in the 1650s.

### *Conclusion*

Although demand for capital investment in industrial and trading concerns was increasing—rapidly when compared with the preceding century—there seems little doubt that the greatest absolute demand for capital investment came from the agricultural sector and that the men who had made their fortunes in industry, trade, farming or government chose to invest most of this capital in land, agriculture, building and conspicuous consumption.

# 5

# Credit

Until the reign of Elizabeth, the English Crown raised most of its loans abroad; as a consequence the London money-market was geared to the requirements of private individuals—the merchant seeking capital for trading voyages; the landowner mortgaging his land to relieve his indebtedness and prevent the necessity of selling his property; the aristocrat or gentleman raising a loan for investment in industrial, mercantile or agricultural enterprise. The subject of the home money-market and, more particularly, of the development of credit facilities during the sixteenth and seventeenth centuries is now seen as of paramount importance. For example, there was a chronic shortage of ready cash in the seventeenth century which coincided with a multiplication of commercial transactions which demanded just such ready money—credit facilities filled the gap and became, as time went on, increasingly sophisticated. Such developments enabled English trade and both industrial and agricultural production to continue to expand. For many years a group of historians (R. H. Tawney, H. Trevor-Roper, J. Hexter, Lawrence Stone and others) were locked in combat regarding the nature of social change in the sixteenth and seventeenth centuries—were the aristocracy in decline? Were the gentry rising to assume the traditional aristocratic role in society? Were some of the gentry prospering and others entering relative decline? Was the prosperity of certain of the gentry due to their landholdings and their superior, adventurous estate management? Were the aristocracy overly conservative in their approach to both land management and industrial and commercial enterprise? In this attempt to find a generalisation which fitted the facts historians were disappointed—perhaps H. Trevor-Roper came closest to the true facts when he said that aristocracy and gentry formed one class and that what one must look for are movements within a class rather than between classes. The controversy, however, did a valuable service in bringing to light much detail concerning the economic ventures of members of the aristocracy and gentry and in bringing increasing sophistication to the historians' techniques in studying such problems. A by-product of the debate was a growing awareness of the importance of credit facilities in enabling 'declining' gentry and aristocracy to stave off final economic defeat, either temporarily or permanently, and in giving others the necessary funds to invest in commercial, industrial or agricultural exploits. Attempts to balance the two uses of credit against one another—to assess the 'decline' of the gentry or aristocracy by estimating the number of gentry or aristocratic families who had to mortgage their property and to see how many finally lost their property to the mortgagee; and to see how many gentry used credit to invest in profitable enterprise—bore little fruit because of inadequate documentation, but were important in demonstrating the truth that the use of credit did not always imply financial difficulties. Even if the attentions of historians are now directed to other problems, it remains true that the economic historian needs to understand the nature of available credit facilities to contemporaries, the pros and cons of their usage, developments in these facilities and in consequent transactions, and the effect upon the organisation of the money-market of Crown borrowing at home.

Usury (money-lending at interest) was a by-employment engaged in by many occupations—notably, merchants, metal-workers (goldsmiths and silversmiths), scriveners, and so on. Recent research on the wills and inventories of persons of all classes has shown that much small-scale lending took place privately between individuals in a very informal way—clergymen, for example, lent parishioners small sums (presumably at interest) and allowed others to pay their annual tithes at some time after the due date, a typical clerical bequest was the forgiveness of such a debt to a parishioner. In an excellent chapter in the *Agrarian History of England and Wales*, Professor Everitt explained that it was the essentially personal conception of credit which was so inadequate in the trading of the farming community—credit meant reputation. A man was tempted to 'engage in dealings beyond his means or worth'; this was fair enough until either customers failed to pay their debts or the harvest failed, when disaster befell the trader. There were no provincial banks—that of Thomas Smith in Nottingham was the only such bank even in the late seventeenth century—yet there was a real need for credit and for the other facilities which a modern bank offers its clients to enable farmers to expand their enterprise.

Most of what historians know of the English money-market in the period concerns the metropolis. It was the port of London and the city crafts and trades which stimulated the growth of an active money-market in the first place and it was with this money-market that the Crown involved itself in the late sixteenth and seventeenth centuries. By the late sixteenth century there was already a highly developed bill market in London. The bill of exchange was perhaps the most common vehicle of mercantile credit: such bills had become increasingly possible after the re-legalisation of interest charges in 1571 (they had been made illegal under Mary). These bills originated for use in foreign trade. For instance, an English merchant might sell a commodity to a Belgian merchant living in Antwerp but might wish to receive payment in England. The Belgian buyer, therefore, would make use of the services of an exchanger in Antwerp—he would pay the exchanger in Flemish money and the exchanger would write a bill of exchange to another exchanger, this time in England, to pay an equivalent sum in English coin to the English seller. The English exchanger would be the Belgian exchanger's business connection in England. The bill of exchange would be payable to the English seller after an interval (specified) which would allow for carriage and for the English exchanger to raise the necessary funds.

Such bills were also extremely useful in enabling English merchants abroad to transfer earned funds back to England without the tedious and difficult task of exporting specie back to England. Englishmen abroad bought bills of exchange, with foreign currency, which were transferred to London and sold to foreign merchants who themselves wished to dispose of sterling earnings. The price of such bills was governed by the current rate of exchange, itself determined by the gold and silver content of the coinage involved and by the current demand for supply of both currencies, and by the prevailing rate of interest, because selling a bill amounted to receiving a short-term loan repayment at a specified later date.

The bill of exchange was essential to commerce because of its convenience as a method of transferring funds rather than because it offered a credit facility—most of the funds necessary for commercial and industrial enterprise came from private investors or, to a very limited extent, from banks such as the Bank of Amsterdam or the Bank of England in the very late seventeenth century. Why was this? Basically it was because the bill of exchange offered few credit advantages to either buyer or seller: it made formal the amount of the debt and stipulated a time and place for payment and no buyer would wish to be tied down to this extent in incurring a debt; it offered little extra security to the seller if he was already satisfied as to the buyer's credit worthiness; the seller of goods on the credit of a bill of exchange had small chance of selling the bill before the payment date was due and making extra money in this way. This was because bills of exchange were difficult to sell. The bill named the payee and the lender was assured of legal help in enforcing payment from him that was named; the principle of assignability of a bill of exchange was not accepted, however, until well into the seventeenth century—bills were endorsed as payable to someone other than the lender before this, but legally there was no protection for the new holder of the bill. Endorsement of bills to persons other than the named creditor became common practice in the mid-seventeenth century but was not legally recognised until the very end of the century. Until this happened the bill of exchange could not be a truly versatile and satisfactory credit vehicle. The bill of exchange was well adapted to a trade situation based on personal connection, but until the early eighteenth century it did not solve the impersonal problem of the trading world, the problem of liquidity.

The early seventeenth century witnessed the development of the true inland bill of exchange as a substitute for the device of dry or fictitious exchange. Prior to 1571 Englishmen wishing to transfer funds internally or to make short-term loans had circumvented the usury laws by means of *dry* or *fictitious* exchanges: the former actually did involve transference of funds in exchange between countries; the latter was merely an interest-bearing loan disguised as an exchange transaction. Gradually the use of bills of exchange replaced such cumbersome devices: landowners who wished to transfer rental receipts to London purchased bills from persons seeking credit, arranging repayment via the debtor's agent or bank in London. The role of the agent or bank in such transactions was all-important—the business of buying and selling bills of exchange was becoming impersonalised as it expanded; the buyer of a bill could not always be sure of the credit worthiness of his new debtor but he was willing to enter into such a transaction if it were backed by a credit-worthy bank or merchant. Once bills became readily assignable to 'the bearer' rather than a named creditor, their attractiveness as a means of transferring funds, earning interest, or making a ready profit was greatly increased. A landowner intending to pay his rents to his London house could revise his decision in favour of ready cash for a provincial venture or in order to pay off one of his own provincial or metropolitan debts by simply assigning the bill.

Useful though bills of exchange became to both foreign and internal affairs they were essentially a means of transferring funds or obtaining short-term loans. Even in the late seventeenth century it was rare for a bill of exchange to take longer than three months to mature. There was, however, a real need for long-term loans, and the use of other credit techniques was widespread. The bond was well suited to the needs of the long-term borrower [23]; there was security for the lender in that the penalty for non-payment within the conditions of the bond was far larger than the principal debt and accrued interest combined, and because the guarantors of repayment provided collateral security. The bond ran for between six and twelve months generally. If the debtor defaulted the creditor found more ready assistance from the common law in enforcing his claim.

Until the 1640s the pledge proved even more attractive to persons willing to lend money—the security offered consisted of either real or personal property which would become the creditor's automatically if the debtor defaulted. Most commonly the pledge took the form of a mortgage on land. Those engaged in money-lending were not slow to foreclose on property after default and mortgaging land became regarded as a last desperate expedient by hard-pressed landowners. The seventeenth century saw increasing sophistication of the mortgage with the introduction of the equity of redemption. This ensured that the defaulting debtor could redeem his foreclosed property by keeping up his due interest payments. This new development was not popular with those lenders who engaged in offering mortgages as a means of speculation on the likely default of the borrower.

Both the bond of obligation and the pledge (mortgage) were best suited to the requirements of the gentry and property-owning classes. Methods of raising long-term capital loans for commercial purposes have been discussed in the last chapter. Before proceeding to discuss the impact of Crown borrowing on the London money-market it is necessary to consider two questions. How extensively were credit facilities used internally? Who offered credit to borrowers?

As already indicated, money-lending was not a specialised occupation in the period. Financial middlemen were a necessity in an impersonalised, countrywide system, as we have seen with relation to the internal bill of exchange. Merchants lent much of their capital but they did so through financial middlemen—the progenitors of modern bankers, estate agents, conveyancers, and solicitors. Much of this business passed through the hands of the scriveners and the goldsmiths. This situation arose because these were men who in the course of their everyday business came into contact with men wealthy enough to want to deposit surplus funds and to earn interest upon them; or wealthy enough to be extravagant and require additional capital to supplement their resources. The goldsmiths also had to provide safe vaults for the precious metals in which they worked and these could be utilised for a bank of deposit [24]. Charles I's raid on the Mint in 1640 caused the wealthy to place their funds with the goldsmiths for safe keeping. Gradually during the course of the third quarter of the seventeenth century the goldsmiths developed three distinct functions—they took deposits; discounted bills; and issued notes. These are functions typical of the modern bank. To what extent these were the dominant business of the goldsmith is doubtful—probably financial dealings of this kind were still a sideline for most.

The issue of notes was an important development. The note was initially a receipt for a deposit promising, on the part of the 'banker', to pay the depositer his money back when claimed with this note. Experience showed the 'bankers' that all depositors did not arrive at one time to demand their funds. This fact enabled bankers to invest some of the money and also to issue a greater volume of money notes than the amount of cash deposited with them. This meant firstly that deposited money was earning interest and secondly that the issue of bank notes was easing the currency shortage in the community. For this reason many economic theorists recommended the establishment of permanent banks because of their social as well as their economic benefits.

The scriveners, also, have been described as pioneers of banking and stock-broking. Professor D. C. Coleman suggested some time ago that whereas the scriveners 'gave assistance to the birth of banking in this country' their activities led them into rather different forms of intermediary work, no less important to the development of the money-market. He studied the surviving business files of a firm of scriveners owned by Robert (later Alderman Sir) Clayton and John Morris. Between 1650 and 1700 the firm's interests covered thirty-nine English counties and several properties in Wales and Ireland; most of the business transacted was in the London, Home Counties area; a Midland belt covering counties from Norfolk and Lincolnshire to Wiltshire and Gloucestershire; and Yorkshire. The work of the firm was varied: particulars of land for sale were obtained and sent to likely purchasers—descriptions made particular play of distance from markets and ports, title, social advantage, and other points relevant to a purchaser [25]; mortgages on property were arranged in a similar fashion—for instance, in 1668 Morris was offered a mortgaged estate of Sir Edward Hales for further mortgage [25]; no evidence exists that Clayton and Morris were also receiving deposits of money or investments from clients but evidence from elsewhere illustrates that scriveners were performing banking and broking functions; the Clayton-Morris files do suggest that the firm was advancing loans for the purposes of investment—in urban rather than agricultural development [25].

There is no suggestion that the Clayton-Morris example is typical—

indeed it probably is atypical in that the firm was extraordinarily large and in that Robert Clayton eventually advanced himself via his work to the position of Lord Mayor of London. Most scriveners probably engaged in such work as essentially a sideline to their normal clerical and legal business. The period after 1539, however, saw a land market which was exceptionally active—the sale of the monastic lands had barely ended before the sequestration, fines and compounding against royalist delinquents and the extensive sales of Crown and Church lands of the Interregnum, and a Restoration settlement which so burdened many returned royalist landowners that they had to sell or mortgage their lands. There was every incentive for scriveners to involve themselves in the work of land agents and to expand this side of their business.

Professor Coleman believes that, at least in the case of Clayton and Morris, the scriveners were often actually the mortgagees who advanced the money to borrowers and eventually foreclosed on their mortgaged property when they defaulted in payment—often predictably. Usually they merely re-sold these lands, although Clayton himself built up a landed estate for himself—reputedly out of the estate of the 2nd Duke of Buckingham. As indicated the scriveners were not normally bankers on a large scale and they seem to have obtained the money for mortgage advances and investment loans from the 'bankers' of the metropolis such as Sir Robert Viner [24].

All in all such evidence suggests that a degree of specialisation had already taken place in the mid-seventeenth century—the goldsmiths appear as the precursors of the modern bank while the scriveners, although participating to a limited extent in the business of banking, were involving their energies more directly in acting as land agents and forming the necessary contacts between land buyers and sellers, mortgagors and mortgagees.

Much work has been done by historians on the fortunes of the landed gentry during the period 1540–1640 and has highlighted the borrowing activities of certain families [26]. Mary Finch, for example, demonstrated how Thomas Tresham built up his inherited estates by resumptions, enclosures and purchases into a great sheep farm between 1559 and 1590 and how penalties for his Catholic recusancy, consequent debarment from State office and removal from direct estate management through imprisonment; the survival of nine children requiring settlements; lavish householding and personal expenditure, served to burden this estate with great debts. She asked the pertinent question whether the instruments of debt and security available were 'sufficiently developed and flexible to enable the slowly accruing profits from the Tresham estate, and the fruits of Sir Thomas's improved management, gradually to reduce and discharge his debts? Or did their limitations predestine his efforts to failure?' Tresham borrowed mainly by bond either on his own security or on that of himself and his friends. He borrowed money from London merchants, financiers and lawyers. Occasionally he was forced to enter into a recognisance permitting the lenders to pursue him by legal process immediately if he defaulted, but it was not until 1589 that he resorted to the device of a mortgage. This was a last desperate resort because he could not raise money by any other means.

The pattern of his borrowing was determined by the fact that what he required prior to 1587 were short-term loans to cover immediate debts and excessive expenditure. Tresham was known to be prosperous and he found it easy to raise credit. In 1587, however, he faced a crisis when recusancy penalties and arrears were enforced; as a result his credit worthiness was greatly impaired. It seemed that he was in danger of forfeiting his obligation—this meant paying a sum at least twice as great as the original debt and it would affect the sureties (persons who had acted as security for his debt) first, meaning that obtaining persons to act as sureties in future would be almost impossible. Clearly keeping one's personal credit reputation intact was all-important if one wished to renew one's borrowing activities—prompt payment was the best means of ensuring this but if this was not possible the borrower would be wise to try to negotiate a fresh loan elsewhere to pay off the first so that credit did not suffer. Tresham's credit was much damaged, but rather than look immediately to the possibility of a mortgage he considered the possibility of selling a rent charge and in fact did grant a redeemable rent charge to raise immediate funds. In 1600 he raised a sum of £500 on a yearly rental of £50 from certain pastures, which he could redeem for £500 at the end of a ten-year period. For some reason Tresham did not make extensive use of this very satisfactory means of raising long-term loans.

When Tresham failed to pay the arrears on his recusancy fines and in consequence the lands of his sureties were seized, his credit received a crippling blow: he was forced to resort to mortgaging his property. He obtained mortgages at least six times between February 1589 and December 1601, apparently at 10 per cent interest. They did have the virtue of providing Tresham with money for a longer period than did the normal bonds which he used but, as earlier explained, they were an 'inconvenient and perilous expedient'. Thomas Colwell foreclosed on one piece of mortgaged land in 1603 and Tresham had no protection, for the equity of redemption had yet to be introduced to convert the perilous mortgage into a vital and relatively safe means of levying long-term loans. In the same crisis period of 1589 Tresham was also tempted to sell some of his property, according to Miss Finch because of the limitations of available credit facilities. He did not sell land at this time, however, although a group of major sales began in 1596.

In his study of the Yorkshire gentry, Dr J. T. Cliffe discusses further the different types of mortgage available in the seventeenth century. In one type property offered as security was conveyed to the lender in fee simply on condition that it be returned to the borrower when the principal sum and the interest had been repaid; normally the mortgagee was allowed to remain in possession of the land and enjoy its produce as long as he kept up with the interest payments. There was a further variety of mortgage agreement: in this the lender received a long lease of the property involved and separately granted the borrower a sublease at a rent corresponding to the interest due on the loan. The advantages of the mortgage prior to the seventeenth century were that they made available to the borrower sums of money for between one and twenty years. The disadvantages have already been touched upon. During Elizabeth's reign the Court of Chancery had offered some protection for borrowers who proved unable to pay the principal because of ill health or theft and in the seventeenth century this protection was offered to all. A number of test cases established that the borrower might redeem his property in Chancery if he paid principal, interest and expenses within a reasonable time after forfeiture. This development took place during the years 1615–30 and was accompanied by a measure which favoured the lenders—they were allowed to secure Chancery decrees ordering payment in full by a set date; if the borrower defaulted at this point the lender could foreclose on the property and possess it in absolute ownership. In Yorkshire at least there is evidence to support Miss Finch's contention that the introduction of the Equity of Redemption promoted greater stability among the landed classes by permitting them the facility of long-term borrowing without the hazards of necessary forfeiture—the number of mortgage loans levied by Yorkshire gentry families rose from 5 between 1600 and 1609 to 55 between 1630 and 1639. Yet Dr Cliffe points out that mortgage borrowing still had its risks—when a borrower failed to pay up at the specified date the lender still had the power to possess and enter the property until it was redeemed; he would draw the fruits of the estate and this could represent a substantial loss of much-needed revenue for the borrower, who was unable to prevent the forecloser exploiting his temporary advantage to the full.

Recent researches indicate that, whereas the larger landowners were certainly not invulnerable to financial crisis during the seventeenth century, they were in a better position to survive the storm with at least the central portion of their lands intact than were the lesser gentry who had annual incomes of perhaps between £50 and £200 per annum. Such men found their estates equally burdened by the costs of wardship, education, improvement, hospitality, and so forth, but found themselves less able to secure loans or to afford the legal fees necessary in attempting to redeem mortgaged property or buy Privy Council letters designed to protect them from the attentions of their creditors.

*Increasing sophistication of the money-market owing to pressure from the Crown*

What has been discussed so far is a money-market geared closely to the requirements of individual merchants on the one hand and of individual landowners on the other. Prior to the sixteenth century most Crown loans had been levied abroad but the reigns of Henry VII and VIII saw a rejection of this policy and a turning to borrowing from wealthy merchants and financiers within the London money-market. Such a policy was not overly successful because of the fact that London was a commercial backwater in comparison with major continental ports and cities; moreover, the attempts to levy loans over a wider spectrum of English society by means of benevolences and forced loans could only be a short-term expedient because the landed classes would not stand for these devices on a permanent basis. The English Crown began, therefore, to turn to Antwerp for its loans—this was a natural focus because Antwerp was then the leading market of northern Europe and the staple for English cloth. There were many disadvantages to borrowing in Antwerp, however: it was expensive, for, although interest rates had fallen from around 14 per cent in the early sixteenth century to 12 per cent under the policy of Sir Thomas Gresham, there were many burdensome overheads which would not have been incurred on the home market such as the expense of maintaining agents in the port, of paying for their travel to various districts in search of lenders, and of transporting funds (either in bullion or coin) from England to Antwerp and vice versa when the exchange system could not be used; secondly, the exchange market was geared to providing short-term credit from one fair to the next for individual merchants whereas the Crown wanted long-term credit—the Antwerp creditors of the Crown were unsympathetic to the Crown's plight and were liable to refuse the Crown renewal of loans and to demand payment at a time when exchange rates or circumstances were unfavourable for the Crown. The Crown normally got round this problem by either playing for time or by borrowing from fresh creditors in order to pay off the immediate loan. This was, to say the least, inconvenient and expensive and it galled the Crown that it could bring no pressure to bear upon foreign financiers either to extend loans or to lend money in the first instance. The native money-market offered far more obvious opportunities for bringing such pressure to bear effectively. When religious conflagration and the withdrawal of foreign staples (including English cloth) from Antwerp occurred and when sheer physical scarcity of money made loans not so much expensive as impossible to secure in that city, the age of flirtation with the Antwerp financiers and merchants was over: in 1574 England cancelled her last remaining monetary obligations abroad.

All was not smooth sailing for the Crown in English waters, however. As we have seen the money-market was geared to the short-term demands of private individuals here as at Antwerp and merchants were not interested in the demands for long-term credit made by the Crown. The prospect of lending to the Crown was made yet more unattractive by the fact that the Crown was immune from the ordinary legal processes which normally a lender might bring to bear upon a defaulter to obtain redress and by the fact that the Crown was trying to secure enormous loans at long term.

To circumvent such problems the Crown under the Early Stuarts did make unsuccessful overtures to German financiers and made use of forced loans on the landed classes by means of Letters of Privy Seal. The Crown was forced to look to the metropolis for most of its loans and those in 1616 of £12,000 and in 1621 of £12,000 from Richard Robartes, the Cornish tin magnate and money-lender, were the exception rather than the rule. Leading Crown favourites made substantial loans to the Crown—in 1624, for instance, the Duke of Buckingham advanced £10,000 towards naval charges and in 1626 he negotiated a loan of £10,000 from the money-lender Sir Paul Bayning. Crown appointments as collectors of government revenue or officials of the main disbursing departments were accompanied by a tacit understanding that the officials would be prepared to make advances to the Crown when asked. As a consequence such men were normally substantial business men. For example, Sir William Russell, merchant financier, was naval treasurer from 1618 to 1627 and from 1630 to 1642, and made notable advances to the Crown both for naval and personal expenditure; Russell received in return the interest on such advances and a large working capital from naval revenue in years when naval costs were not heavy enough to eat the revenue up. Similarly the farmers of the Customs revenue, particularly of the Great Customs, were prominent as individual lenders to the government. The Crown also made considerable use of the services of alien financiers resident in London. The most notable example is that of Philip Burlamachi who during the 1620s allowed the Crown to use his own substantial credit abroad and who after 1624 made large loans to the Crown and often acted as paymaster of the English troops on the Continent. In 1633 his bankruptcy was caused by the government's failure to repay long-standing loans to him. Sir Baptist Hicks was a native English financier who was also prepared to advance money to the Crown for long periods. The financial demands of the Crown were so enormous, however, that they could not be met by the resources of ordinary money-lenders and men like Burlamachi, Pindar, Russell, Vanlore and Courteen were few and far between.

The Crown overcame this problem of the shortage of available funds by developing the use of the loan syndicate. This took three major forms: an ad hoc combination of individual lenders [27]; a group of merchants; or a body of government concessionaires, such as the Farmers of the Great Customs or the Contractors for the purchase and re-sale of Crown lands or a monopolistic company such as the Soap-boilers! The Customs farmers, for example, were leased the Customs revenue for a specified period on the understanding that they paid the Crown a given sum per annum. The farmers were willing to advance loans to the Crown amounting to the annual revenue of the farm at no interest until the reign of Charles I—thus, although the lease terms of the farm were soon outdated (as commercial conditions changed) and the Crown was suffering, the favourable economic opportunities thus offered to the farmers made them the more willing to advance long-term loans to the Crown at no interest.

The Crown also used the Corporation of London to secure loans levied on inhabitants of the wards, or the livery companies, or on small groups of aldermen on terms arranged by the government. In some circumstances the Corporation acted as a guarantor for the Crown's limited foreign borrowing. Many of the contributions towards loans on the City were paid into the Chamber of London and on occasion the Chamber would make advances on loans granted to the Crown or underwrite loans if there was a deficiency. The Crown's strained relations with the City of London in the 1630s and 40s had, therefore, dire financial consequences.

The seventeenth century saw the Crown raising extraordinary revenue to finance its foreign policy or to finance its non-parliamentary government. When the Parliament made grants of subsidies to cover war expenses the proceeds were slow to come in and the Crown needed to make immediate use of its revenue—in consequence anticipatory loans were made. In June 1628, for instance, Parliament granted Charles I five subsidies over two years and in that same month the Privy Council lent £9,600 on the revenue of subsidy number one to supply the fleet intended to relieve La Rochelle [28]; in July 1628 a loan of £5,000 was written off against subsidy number three's revenue. In addition the Crown also found it necessary to anticipate its ordinary revenue in order to bridge its deficits and manage the debt arising out of these deficits in terms of interest, wages, and pressing debts. Although it was cheaper to allow debts to accumulate than to incur fresh debts to pay earlier ones off, the Crown was forced to borrow anew in order to maintain its creditability. Postponement of debt was common practice but the Crown utilised subsidy payments to pay off much of its debts [27]—for instance, between 1606 and 1610 the debt was reduced from £735,000 to £280,000 by money from subsidies and the sale of royal woods and lands. It is significant that such moneys were employed to reduce the debt itself rather than to bridge the deficit between income and expenditure or to pay interest on the debt. The Crown looked to loans to do this—it hypothecated future revenues against these new loans. In 1628 £325,000 of the debt had been covered by hypothecating Crown revenue up to two years ahead. During the early 1630s there was a very gradual reduction of this burden by the spreading out of hypothecation, thus by August 1630 some revenues were hypothecated down to 1637; the year 1634, however, saw an alarming rise in the practice of hypothecation. This practice was a very dangerous one in the political climate of the day. In 1639 the Crown was raising fresh loans anticipating loans which Parliament *might* make when it met. Parliament proved intractable. The calling of the Long Parliament marked the beginning of parliamentary control of government borrowing.

The Crown faced great problems in levying long-term loans, as has already been indicated. The Crown's credit was not good and prospective lenders were put off by the fact that the Crown was legally inviolable. Some loans were levied by the use of Letters Patent or Letters of Privy Seal but creditors disliked these because the letters made no mention of the borrower's obligation to pay a penalty on default. Creditors preferred instead to obtain tallies of assignment in return for advances—these tallies when presented to the relevant government office at a specified date would be exchanged for a stipulated share of the office's revenue and a bond assured the creditor only that such tallies would be honoured if there existed available revenue. Creditors ran an additional risk in that the Crown abused the device by over-assigning the revenues in this manner. Borrowing by bond was also disadvantageous to creditors —the lender was unable to sue for penalty when the Crown defaulted and as a consequence was forced to agree to prolongation of the loan involved. Government guarantors, however, were not protected by legal inviolability and in order to obtain sureties the Crown often had to use pressure.

Why then did persons lend to the Crown? Becoming a Crown creditor had its economic and social compensations. For example, the Farmers of the Customs obtained excellent economic opportunities; in 1628 Maxwell was granted a valuable licence to export calf-skins apparently in return for a money advance to Charles I; the aliens Burlamachi and Vandeputt obtained the right to trade on the same advantageous terms as Englishmen by acting as government lenders. Various eminent financiers received titles as a reward for monetary services to the Crown—for instance in 1628 Baptist Hicks was created 1st Viscount Campden and Sir Paul Bayning became Viscount Bayning of Sudbury. On occasion those who had lent money to the Crown would be relieved of their own debts to the Crown: Burlamachi exchanged a loan of £20,000 to the Crown in 1620 for forgiveness of a fine of £4,000 for extortion of specie. Sometimes the methods of inducement were less favourable to the lenders —some royal officials were blackmailed because they had extorted excessive fees from citizens; on one occasion James I gaoled a brewer who failed to advance him with beer supplies on credit. The Crown did try to maintain its credit, such as it was, by punctiliously observing its interest obligations but this became increasingly difficult to do.

The Crown faced financial collapse in the early 1640s but the seeds of this collapse are traceable even as far back as 1611. The precarious financial stability of the 1630s had been dependent upon the maintenance of peace, because the process of cumulative hypothecation which the Crown so much relied on was bound to break down under extraordinary pressure, and because the Crown had neglected to maintain its credit in the City of London so that its funds were no longer available as a source of loans in case of emergency.

Although under the Commonwealth and the Protectorate government sources of revenue were revolutionised by the introduction of the Excise and the Land Tax, the new government approached the money-market in search of loans using much the same devices as its Stuart predecessors —anticipation of the revenues being its mainstay. Whereas the Customs were originally put into commission, towards the end of Cromwell's rule as Protector a move was made to reintroduce the Farm of the

Customs because of its promise of greater profitability. Cromwell found it exceptionally difficult to levy loans at all, either in the City Chamber or from the City Companies—those that he did secure were short-term loans backed by real sureties. The government did make use of several novel devices, however. For example, Debentures or treasury orders were awarded in the 1650s to soldiers for payment of their arrears on such occasion as the government had funds to cover them. Originally these debentures were not assignable but they became so. The Long Parliament had also introduced a method of forcible public borrowing backed by the security of public-faith bills which were in practice of little value. Attempts to forge public-faith bills suggest that they were to some extent redeemable but also gave the government grounds for delaying payment when they were presented.

At the Restoration a settlement was made upon the Crown of a hereditary income on 1.2 million pounds in exchange for customary and feudal dues. For its revenues the Crown was now dependent upon the Customs, the Excise, and the new Hearth Tax of 1662, plus the Assessment, special aids (such as those granted against the Dutch in 1664–5, and 1666) and the Land Tax which was introduced in 1677. Increasing reliance upon revenue from taxation brought its own problems—the income rarely reached the projected sum and was always delayed in collection. Moreover, it was an irregular source of income. The tax farmers had the job of timing the royal income—the Customs were farmed down to 1671; the Excise was farmed until 1683, and the Hearth Tax was farmed from 1667 to 1684 and through the Farmers the Government was able to anticipate the revenue from these taxes and to secure loans. Such methods of deficit finance were, as has been shown, traditional but there was a significant difference. Although the old stalwarts of the Customs farms continued to be prominent in financing government loans a newer breed of men had appeared—the goldsmith bankers such as Noell, Vyner, Backwell and Duncomb. These men advanced money to the Crown out of the proceeds of their private banking business and the system apparently worked well until the Crown found it impossible to collect taxes because of war, plague and fire—at this juncture the debt itself was much increased, the interest payments were behindhand and the bankers became more indispensable and more detested.

According to a zealous public servant such as George Downing, Secretary to the Treasury Commissioners from 1667 to 1672, the King's profligate generosity and extravagance had to be curbed and reliance upon the bankers minimised. He recommended that, in future, parliamentary aids be appropriated to a specific purpose. He also advocated that an appeal for loans be addressed to the public at large, on the understanding that the first to advance money would be the first to be repaid, and on the understanding that repayment orders be assigned so that the lender might receive repayment, after deduction of appropriate discount, at any time if he chose to present his order to a banker. The significant feature of the project was that the public should be encouraged, by discriminatory measures, to place their money directly with the Exchequer rather than via the bankers. The scheme of the National Exchequer bank was based upon Downing's observation of the Dutch system but it failed because government credit was destroyed by the Stop of the Exchequer of 1672 when the Crown renounced its obligation to pay back loans already made to the Exchequer. Most of the orders for repayment had already been discounted by the banks, five of which collapsed as a result of the financial burden they were made to bear. Even the large bankers, such as Vyners and Backwells, went bankrupt in the mid 1680s. The Crown came by accident to found a funded debt—no attempt was made to repay the principal of the loans but annuities were paid to the banks to pay interest or 'annuities' to the borrowers.

It was in the late 1680s that a financial crisis again hit the government —in the year 1689 William III engaged in war. The main source of government revenue from taxation came from the Land Tax although both the Excise and the Customs yield had risen. Between 1688 and 1702 the yield of the Land Tax amounted to £19.1 million while Customs brought in £13.3 million, the Excise some £13.6 million and the Poll Tax £2.6 million. Altogether government revenue from taxation amounted to £58.7 million, as compared with expenditure of £72 million. The country was prosperous enough to bear this increased burden of taxation and improved revenue collection through commissioners helped the government's position but there remained a deficit of just over £13.5 million to be covered by loan.

Many projects to secure government loans were advanced. In 1693 the government founded the first National Debt. This worked on the principles accidentally discovered in 1672. £1,000,000 was to be borrowed. Individual subscribers had a choice: they could take a straightforward annuity of 14 per cent per annum for life, tax free, or take a risk, accept 10 per cent annuity until 1700 and thereafter share in the profits of a fund which had fewer demands to meet as original subscribers died off. The annuities were to be funded by new excise duties on beer and other liquors, separately entered in the Exchequer. The principle was clear that the lender would not again see his capital; moreover, his surety was not the word of the monarch but an Act of Parliament guaranteeing his annuity for life, which would heavily penalise government servants who failed to observe its terms. Other projects were discredited. A Million Lottery established in 1692 came to nothing and temporarily brought into disrepute the sweepstake method of raising loans. The idea of founding a land bank was also frequently broached—this seemed natural as land was by far the most secure investment during the seventeenth century. Such a projected land bank was that of John Briscoe, to which subscriptions were invited in 1695 on the principle that 'England itself was the best fund or security'. Within just over a month in the summer of 1695 subscriptions to a value of £51,438 per annum had been received and it was hoped to raise eventually £100,000 per annum, to which end subscription books were displayed at chambers in Lincoln's Inn, the Inner Temple and Gray's Inn. If the goldsmith bankers of the city were unpopular, there was yet a feeling that there were too few banks. Banks were believed to perform a public good—they eased the acute shortage of money and, from the 1650s on, men like Samuel Hartlib were advocating the foundation of banks both to advance credit and offer deposit facilities to merchants and businessmen and also to facilitate the government's task of transmitting funds (particularly the produce of taxes) from one place to another. Merchants and businessmen would be able to launch ambitious projects which would prove of benefit to the poor by providing work. The value of land would rise as the availability of money was eased and interest rates lowered.

The Bank of England which was established in 1694, however, was not a land bank as favoured by numerous pamphleteers but a combination of commercial bank and source of government borrowing. An Act of Parliament allocated duties on ships' tonnage and other commodities to pay interest of 8 per cent on a loan of £1,200,000. Subscribers were also permitted to borrow money on parliamentary security; to deal in bullion and bills of exchange; and to act as a pawnbroker. The Bank's position as to the issue of notes was left vague. By late 1694 the Bank had loaned most of its funds to the State, the funds (in bills) were deposited in the Exchequer, and tallies were then distributed to pay creditors. The creditor had a choice of action: he could immediately redeem his tally at the bank; he could deposit the tally; he could accept a Bank note in return for the tally. The position appeared risky as the Bank had to issue an equivalent number of Bank notes on the security of the Exchequer tallies alone, but the Bank did weather the storm because of the support of both native and foreign (particularly Dutch) investors.

Until this time the governments had always distrusted the idea of establishing a national bank—indeed, as has been pointed out, Sweden was the only mid-century monarchy to possess one. The founding of the bank, however, 'brought government borrowing under direct control of the representatives of the propertied', involving the moneyed classes intimately in politics, enabling the accumulation of capital and completing the process begun under Cromwell when, by channelling the proceeds of all taxes except the assessment into the Exchequer, a policy of treasury control of both income and expenditure and planned loans first seemed feasible.

The economy of Tudor and Stuart England, becoming increasingly complex, created a demand for more and more sophisticated credit facilities for both small- and large-scale business transactions; for the conduct of internal and external trade; for the financing of improvement ventures and speculative projects; and for the financing of government. The political vicissitudes of the Stuart monarchy contributed to its shaking of public trust and, as a consequence, made it increasingly difficult for the Crown to raise loans to pay for government. Ironically, it was partially the sharp memory of Stuart policies which produced a bank which provided finance and security for government but also a potential vehicle for the control of government activity via the purse.

# 6

# The Plunder of the Church

In 1535 the gross annual value of the monastic lands of England and Wales was probably about £200,000 (or approximately one-quarter of the total landed wealth of the kingdom). It was not surprising that an impecunious and ambitious monarch should turn his attention to this wealth. The story of the dissolution of first the lesser and then the greater monastic foundations in 1536 and 1539 respectively is a very familiar one. In the past historians have portrayed this suppression of the monasteries as the most notable of Henry VIII's pillaging activities consequent upon his rejection of the Roman supremacy. More recently, the work of Professor Joyce Youings and others has demonstrated the orderly, methodical and moderate means by which the monasteries were suppressed. More important yet has been the suggestion that the plunder of the monastic houses was by no means simply an impulsive, anti-papal, avaricious act but an integral part of a carefully conceived if never realised plan for the reorganisation of the Crown's finances.

Historians have been deceived into believing the suppression of the monasteries to be haphazard because so small a proportion of the total of confiscated property was annexed permanently to the Crown's estate, most of it being sold or granted away during the years following. However, it is clear that Thomas Cromwell intended that the monastic lands should become part of the royal estate; pressure of circumstances (wars, political considerations, internal security) confounded this plan. It is also apparent that Cromwell had hoped to plunder the wealth of the entire church in England, in its secular as well as its monastic aspects. The great survey of ecclesiastical wealth, the *Valor Ecclesiasticus* of 1535, encompassed the wealth of bishops, deans and chapters, archdeacons, rectors and vicars as well as of religious foundations. Reformers and opportunist laymen alike were openly discussing the question in the 1530s even before the dissolution got under way. Professor Stone has drawn attention to a project of autumn 1534 whereby the bishops were to be permitted to retain a 'sufficiency' for the support of their official positions and the State was to collect the remainder of their revenues. At this juncture a figure of 2,000 marks for the Archbishop of Canterbury, of 1,000 marks for the other bishops was suggested; later a sum of £1,000 was suggested for the Primate of all England. The episcopate escaped in 1536 when the lesser foundations were dissolved, but in 1536–7 a petition of both Houses was composed asking for the confiscation of both monastic and episcopal surplus wealth, which demanded that neither archbishops nor bishops be allowed more than £1,000 per annum. It envisaged not mass confiscation of monastic property but the death of monasticism by slow strangulation. The petition proposed that the proceeds of this mulcting of the bishops be employed for the defence of the realm and administered by a new court, situated at Coventry in an attempt to revive the fortunes of that town.

It is probable that this petition was not the project of a government minister but of Thomas Gibson, a follower of Latimer. It was not an isolated proposal. In 1539 politicians were voicing similar ideas. Clergy and laity in Lincolnshire during the Pilgrimage of Grace feared that Cromwell would turn his unwanted attentions to their incomes and to the wealth of the parish churches. Bishops such as John Clerk of Bath and Wells, humanist scholar and former colleague of Cromwell, thought it necessary to attempt to propitiate Cromwell with grants and fawning letters.

What saved the bishops seems to have been a difference in approach to the problem on the part of Henry and Cromwell. Cromwell saw an attack on episcopal wealth as a means of placing the royal finances on a new and secure foundation and was more willing to attack episcopal wealth than monastic. Henry was rather more conservative and undecided, seeing the bishops as essential propagandists of his righteous cause. He would be prepared to mulct the sees in order to found new, modestly-endowed dioceses on a county basis, if he had the support of the Catholic bishops. Six of the 13 new bishoprics were eventually established. But when in 1539 a draft bill was drawn up proposing an attack on episcopal riches which were thought unnecessary and spiritually damaging for the Church, the King's response was unfavourable. The King, under the terms of the bill, would have supplied the bishops with land necessary for their support, using the surplus for new endowments. Cathedral, collegiate and chantry lands, however, would have been added to the Crown's estate. A thorough inquiry into ecclesiastical fees was to have been organised. The bill was never brought before Parliament because of the King's hesitancy when faced with such a radical step. Like the Stuart kings he was acutely aware of the need of the Church for material wealth if it were to retain the respect and allegiance of the people and prove a valuable political ally to the Crown, and he was, of course, also aware of his need for support from the Catholic bishops in his confrontation with the papacy.

Henry, of course, did stoop to some plunder of the resources of the episcopate. The case of Canterbury's 'Great Exchange' is a case in point. As Professor Robin Du Boulay has shown, by the end of Henry's reign the original endowment of the see of Canterbury was much depleted by forced grants to the Crown; new lands were annexed to the see, some on a permanent and some on a temporary basis. Although Cranmer to some extent was able to reorganise the administration of the see's estates because of consolidation through exchanges, predominantly the pattern was that the King took what he wanted and Cranmer claimed what he could in recompense. He had to combat not only the King's avarice but also the plans of Cromwell and the new surveyors and auditors for plunder of the bishoprics. For example, one large grant of land from Canterbury to the Crown passed almost immediately into the hands of the chancellor of the Court of Augmentations. By 1546, when all the exchanges had taken place, the total annual income of the see had been reduced by approximately £277. The seriousness of Canterbury's financial predicament was inevitably heightened by rising prices. In 1552 Cranmer bewailed the fact that as archbishop he had a lower standard of living than as a scholar at the university because in spite of a much reduced income he still had heavy responsibilities as archbishop and was expected to maintain the ancient hospitality.

Henry VIII's inconsistent attitude towards the wealth of the English Church was in fact to set a pattern for his successors. No fundamental reform was implemented whereby episcopal lands were centrally administered and the bishops paid a salary by the State; on the other hand the bishops suffered from the spasmodic plundering of their inheritance at the hands of Crown and courtiers.

Although Cromwell's attempts to completely reorganise the Crown's finances were defeated, he did modify the system considerably by his ecclesiastical ventures. Professor F. C. Dietz calculated that the revenues of the Crown from ordinary pre-Cromwellian sources amounted to some £100,000 a year (this excluded extraordinary parliamentary grants and revenues collected and spent locally in Calais, Berwick and Ireland). The new revenues from the Church changed the picture considerably. Until the dissolution of the monasteries, the Crown was collecting first-fruits and tenths from religious foundations and ecclesiastical benefices alike. From 1535 to 1540 these brought in an annual average of £16,000 (a sum greater than the annual revenue from the Duchy of Lancaster and considerably larger than that collected from the Court of Wards). The dissolution of the monastic foundations in 1539 meant a steep fall in this new income—the yield fell to £9,700 a year with the loss of the larger monasteries. Cromwell was aware of the problem but the King could not have it both ways. The gross yield of the annual tenth granted by the clergy likewise fell dramatically. An average income of £29,400 a year from 1535 to 1538 was reduced to but £18,400 a year after the closure of the larger houses, although the new holders of monastic land were still obliged to pay tenths. There were, of course, other financial gains from the Reformation in England—the extraordinary income from the fine on the clergy for offences against the Statute of Praemunire, for example. More regular but still 'extraordinary' grants of money were made by the clergy in the form of subsidies. The Houses of Convocation had the right to grant such a tax to the Crown, although it had to be approved by Parliament. The subsidy rate varied: in 1540, for example, it was assessed at four shillings in the pound of every pound's income of an ecclesiastical benefice after the deduction of the annual tenth; in 1545 the rate was at six shillings in the pound. The subsidies were collected over a given period, of two to four years, specific dates being set for various parts of the payment. The accounts of the treasurer of first-fruits and tenths indicate that the subsidy grossed £24,000 in 1540 and that from then until the end of Henry VIII's reign an annual average of £18,000 was yielded. Approximate figures for the income of the court of first-fruits and tenths are £52,200 per annum plus an income of £18,000 per annum from clerical subsidies. This amounted to half as much again as the Crown's ordinary annual revenue prior to 1540. The increase appears the more staggering when one recalls that the Tudors' receipts from clerical taxation prior to the Reformation had amounted to but £12,500 per year, of which £9,000 had come from clerical subsidies.

One might conclude correctly that whereas Thomas Cromwell was never able to implement the complete takeover of ecclesiastical wealth that he had envisaged, what he did achieve in the sphere of augmenting the royal finances from ecclesiastical resources was still extremely significant.

Examining the 'plunder' of the Church in this context—of a radical desire to command the resources of both monastic foundations and episcopal sees—does not mean that we have to accept the old view that with the proceeds Cromwell hoped to set up a Tudor Despotism, supported by a large standing army. Certainly any hope of having a truly state-controlled church was confounded by the situation in the year before the great dissolution—in 1538 there was a fear of imminent invasion from the Franco-Imperial alliance and a consequent need for great expenditure on erection of fortifications and harbours. This activity demanded large amounts of ready money and immediate confiscation of monastic resources provided just this. Gradual elimination of monasticism and assumption of monastic resources by the Crown was made impossible by the military situation. Because of the radical approach to the regular foundations, a concerted attack upon episcopal wealth did not seem timely.

Even before this it had always been intended that some monastic estates should be sold or granted away from the Crown. After the major dissolution of 1539 the dispersal of monastic lands by the Crown became the norm. Commissions were issued for the sale of land up to a given total value by the Crown [29]. The first such commission was made to Sir Richard Rich and Thomas Cromwell in December of 1539 to sell lands to the total annual value of £6,000 for ready money. The land was to be sold at a rate of twenty times the current net annual value of the land. Land in towns could be sold at a lesser rate. Indications are that a rate of 20 years' purchase was already normal in those grants of monastic land made since the first spate of dissolutions.

The initiative for the sale of a particular piece of property always came from the prospective purchaser and not from the Crown or its commissioners. The grantee had first to obtain a *valor* of the desired property from the appropriate auditor of augmentations [30]; then the commissioners appended their own 'rating' of the property which was based upon the net value of the property after the deduction of the annual tenth reserved to the Crown, the value of lands or property being offered in exchange, and any royal grants and concessions from the transaction. The rating made no account of buildings still in position on the site. On top of the rate of twenty times this net sum were added lump charges for woods (which were separately surveyed) and for advowsons or rights of presentation to ecclesiastical livings appended to the property. The commissioners added stipulations concerning the time in which the purchase price was to be paid, and signed the ratings. The purchaser completed the transaction by entering a signed and sealed request for purchase on the terms previously settled. Such a transaction took a considerable time to complete as the auditors and commissioners went about their tasks in leisurely fashion, before a royal warrant for the transaction was procured.

Considerable research has been done into the market for this monastic property. At one time the fact that the same men were continually appearing as grantees for monastic estates was believed to indicate that there was a group of speculators in monastic property. This conclusion was supported by the fact that much of the land so purchased was almost immediately disposed of to other purchasers in much smaller parcels. Recently, however, it has been argued convincingly that the habitual buyers of monastic property, particularly those who purchased carefully-selected properties in many different areas of England and obtained licences for their immediate alienation, were rather the agents of other prospective purchasers. The need for agents of this kind seems obvious —not every would-be landowner knew what to do to obtain a grant; had the courage to initiate proceedings in the Court of Augmentations; or could afford the lengthy stays in the capital necessary to put through even a trivial transaction. Most of the transactions enacted by these men were performed in their capacity as agents—however, it may be that historians are now being led to underestimate the activities of the few speculators who did exist and, certainly, some buyers used their purchases as a form of patronage—dispensing with monastic lands to friends and clients.

Dr Outhwaite has argued that in the reign of Elizabeth most real purchasers (as opposed to patentees who were agents or attorneys for true purchasers) were making modest purchases of monastic land through the Crown and that, moreover, most of their purchases reflected essentially localised interests. Three sales of Crown property in 1589–90, 1599, and 1601 were studied in detail and it was found that in each of the sales the proportion of purchasers who bought land in one county only amounted to 80 per cent and that, if purchases in two adjacent counties are included, the percentage of essentially local transactions rises to 90 per cent. Most of the actual purchasers belonged to the gentry classes, although the yeomanry also participated to a significant extent. The pattern of their purchases suggests that the buyers' interest was predominantly in consolidating existing holdings and buying neighbouring properties. Few true purchasers demonstrated any interest in buying geographically widely-scattered properties. His findings also suggest that most purchasers bought land from the Crown on one occasion only—the lists of patentees for all three sales yield the names of 800 individuals: only 7 had ratings drawn up in all three sales; 27 had property rated in the first two sales; 5 in the first and the last; 21 in the last two. It is clear that the names of agents are prominent in this group and the reasons for the multiple purchases of several of the others can be accounted for by their determination to achieve a consolidation of estate in a given area.

Under Elizabeth the attractiveness of buying land from the Crown was somewhat diminished. This was mainly because a great many of the existing leases on Crown property were reversionary—prospective purchasers of Crown lands had to face the fact that they might not be able to reap the profits of the land for several 'lives' because the Crown had already granted leases in the future. Elizabeth realised that the existence of reversionary leases was depressing the marketability, if not the market price, of Crown lands and is supposed to have resisted courtiers' petitions for further such grants in an attempt to stop the rot. Also, rents and charges on Crown lands had remained unchanged for years—unless the purchaser was prepared to wait for the existing lease to lapse or to buy out the lessees, he could not revise these rents, and he might meet considerable opposition from those who had previously been protected by the Crown in their position.

From Elizabeth's point of view this situation was unfortunate but in so far as monastic estate was concerned by no means dramatic: after all by the end of Henry VIII's reign over half of the monastic property had already been dispersed and by the time of Elizabeth's accession but a quarter remained to her use.

The second dissolution had abolished monasticism in England and Wales—the economic plunder of the religious houses was complete. The bishops and secular clergy, however, remained to suffer the effects of depleted resources. Many historians have laid the blame for the precarious financial condition of the English episcopate at the door of the Crown—certainly, as Professor J. J. Scarisbrick has shown, the clergy as a whole were far more heavily taxed by the Crown after 1535 than they had been by both Crown and papacy prior to the Reformation and, moreover, the burden of taxation upon the clergy was apparently proportionately much heavier than that borne by the laity. Apart from this, however, historians are rapidly becoming more and more aware of the fact that the role of the Crown as predator of episcopal resources has been over-emphasised in the past. This seems particularly so in the case of Elizabeth.

For example, the total annual income of the twenty-six mainland sees of England during Elizabeth's reign, according to available statistics, remained unchanged from beginning to end of the reign.* As will be demonstrated later, this does not mean that the real value of the annual receipts remained unaltered, but such developments were normally out-

* According to more recent tentative statistics produced by Dr Felicity Heal, the total value of the English and Welsh sees did fall slightly during this period, from £27,250 to £25,100.

side the Crown's province. What can be said is that Elizabeth was generally (but not always) in practice unsympathetic to the need for *augmentation* of episcopal resources during hard times, even if she did not actually engage in plunder of their existing resources. Of course, it is true that the annual receipts of *individual* bishoprics had changed—the effect was that the wealth of the episcopate was now rather more evenly balanced, with wealthy sees such as Winchester and Durham being forced to surrender property to the Crown, and the poorer sees being left intact.

A traditional charge against Elizabeth has been that she left sees vacant for considerable periods of time in order to reap their profits *sede vacante*. The charge is groundless if applied to her initial appointments—delays here were caused by difficulties in finding suitable candidates. Three vacancies (those in Bristol and Oxford for most of the reign, and at Ely for some nineteen years) may have had a financial motivation; otherwise only six times were sees (Bath and Wells—twice; Chichester; Gloucester; Llandaff; and Salisbury) left vacant for more than two years. Yet closer examination suggests that, had Elizabeth really been seeking financial remuneration via extended vacancies, she could have chosen more promising subjects—both Bristol and Oxford were among the poorly-endowed Henrician sees and, in any event, the income of Bristol was for a good part of the vacancy held *in commendam* by the Bishop of Gloucester and not by the Crown at all; Gloucester and Llandaff were both poor sees; Bath and Wells and Chichester were moderately prosperous but had already suffered heavily at the Crown's hands under Edward VI and Somerset; Salisbury was relatively wealthy. The prolonged vacancy at Ely may be ascribed to a non-financial motive—it appears that Archbishop Whitgift as ordinary *sede vacante* of the university sees of both wealthy Ely and impoverished Oxford was able to deal directly with problems arising out of the universities, at a time when Puritanism at Cambridge in particular was causing much trouble.

The Crown was certainly not unaware of the fact that revenue from episcopal first-fruits was valuable—representing as it did a full year's revenue (minus the tenths) of the sees concerned. In 1575 a list was prepared demonstrating how the Queen might profit financially by translating bishops from one see to another at fairly frequent intervals, thus stepping up the occurrence of first-fruits. Lord Keeper Puckering showed how the successive moves of five bishops would bring in a handsome profit to the Crown. The Crown never implemented these suggestions. Some 35 per cent of Elizabeth's episcopal appointments after the initial spate in 1558–62 were translations from one see to another. Not until the nineteenth century was the rate again to be so low. Moreover, the types of translation involved were scarcely the most lucrative—they involved moves from poor sees to moderate sees; only six bishops were translated to third sees which produced more profit in terms of first-fruits. The early Stuarts, on the other hand, might far more fairly be accused of adopting this practice—twelve men were appointed to third sees; two of these were translated to fourth dioceses and one, Richard Neile, held six bishoprics in all.

Christopher Hill has charged Elizabeth with being 'Supreme Plunderer' as well as 'Supreme Governor' of the Church of England. Recent case studies of various English sees indicate that this charge is groundless. As we have seen, the lands of Canterbury were pillaged by Henry VIII in a series of eight exchanges between 1536 and 1547; in 1542 Edward Lee, Archbishop of York, was persuaded to sell to the Crown four archiepiscopal manors in return for a cash sum and fourteen separate assignments of ex-monastic land and advowsons. Lee's successor, Robert Holgate, was only elevated to the primacy at the cost of a massive alienation of land in 1545 which was recompensed very unequally by a grant of some thirty-nine rectories formerly appropriated to Yorkshire's monastic foundations. Other large grants were made to the Crown and, although the Crown made some concession to the archiepiscopal see in acknowledgement of the decrease in its revenue, amounting to a reduction in first-fruits by almost one-half of the initial assessment prior to 1545, the financial fortunes of the see were at a very low ebb indeed at the end of Henry's reign. Dr Claire Cross, however, has made it clear that the threat to York's possessions was removed by Henry's demise. Edward's reign saw no further plunder of the estates and Queen Mary gave positive help to her Archbishop of York, Nicholas Heath, by releasing him and his successors from rental payments due on the lands and rectories granted to the see by Henry VIII—a saving of some £258 7s. per annum—and, more significantly, by restoring to the see three of its important pre-Reformation lordships. In 1559 York was again a well-endowed see but, despite the fact that Elizabeth ordered a survey of York and other sees with a view to enforcing exchanges of property, the see escaped any such plunder. Indeed, during Elizabeth's reign threats to episcopal property came less from the Queen than from courtiers such as Leicester. The reign of James I saw the last of the exchanges of York episcopal property with the Crown—in 1622 a relatively minor exchange took place when Archbishop Toby Matthew surrendered York House to the King in return for four Yorkshire manors. Viewed over the century as a whole, the Henrician exchanges combined with the Marian restorations meant that the total annual income of the see of York was little affected, although by the late sixteenth century its economic basis was much different because the income was now drawn increasingly from impropriations as opposed to temporal manors.

Evidence for the sees of Lincoln, Exeter and Bath and Wells suggests that they suffered their worst period of depredation under the rule of Edward Tudor. The ascendancy of Somerset was particularly damaging for Bath and Wells. The Protector's attentions were turned to the episcopal lands because he had already made considerable acquisitions of property in Somersetshire and wished to consolidate his territorial position in the west. Just as the new Bishop of Lincoln was making grants to the Protector, so the Bishop of Bath and Wells, Barlow, found himself in 1548 surrendering to Somerset Wells itself, six other episcopal manors, and other property—a bloc described by Dr Phyllis Hembry as 'the very heart of the see'. Both the Bishop of Lincoln and the Bishop of Bath were also making considerable grants of property to the Crown itself. Historians have attributed to Mary a desire to restore alienated episcopal lands—the case of York, for example, bears this out—but in the case of Bath and Wells she demonstrated no such tendency. Some restitution of episcopal property was certainly accorded the Marian bishop, Gilbert Bourne, in that the important manor of Banwell was restored to him, but this was most heavily burdened so that the net profit from it to the bishopric was negligible in some years.

The case of the see of Ely is a rather different one. Its recent historian—Dr Felicity Heal—has confessed that during the unprecedented nineteen-year vacancy of the see from 1581 to 1600, the revenues of the see were utilised by the Crown in support of the costly Spanish war—it was reported that a pension was paid to the King of Portugal from this source. Financial difficulties during the 1590s made it all the more tempting to leave the diocese vacant and overrode Puckering's scheme for the profitable translation of five bishops referred to earlier. When a bishop, Martin Heaton, was appointed, the act was dictated by financial considerations—the price of his elevation was a colossal exchange of episcopal property involving thirty-four of the see's remaining manors. As at York, a changed foundation for the see's revenue was the result: prior to 1559 only a tiny fraction of the annual receipts were drawn from spiritualities such as impropriations and tithes; even after the exchange of lands to the Crown of 1559 only one-third of income was drawn from such sources; yet by 1608 about half of the episcopal revenue came from spiritualities rather than temporalities. That Elizabeth's attitude to Ely was predatory cannot be denied but Dr Heal reminds us that the financial consequences of this policy were less damaging than might have been expected. Elizabeth released the bishops of Ely from the obligation to pay tenths on their property after 1559, which represented a saving in expenditure of £207. Moreover, as Ely had escaped the worst of Edward's depredations, the pillaging of Elizabeth's reign had a less marked effect on episcopal ability to pay its way. An estimate of the money income of the see between 1454 and 1608 suggests that total receipts had fallen by only about £200 since 1535.

In a recent discussion of the Act of Exchanges of 1559, Dr Heal has suggested that initially Cecil saw the project as one which would involve a major rationalisation of episcopal finances. The reform lost momentum as several factors emerged. Neither the Crown nor a majority of the episcopal bench wished to see a new type of non-political bishop. The workings of the Act were too slow and cumbersome to render it worthwhile. There were too many special cases; too many very poor sees; too much episcopal and parliamentary opposition; too much hard work and expense was involved in surveying episcopal property and setting up commissions. Thus the image of the Crown and particularly of Elizabeth as 'supreme plunderer' of the episcopate seems shaken. Except for a brief period, even in 1559 Elizabeth did not contemplate further ravaging of the poorer dioceses. The initial exchanges involved Canterbury, London, Ely, Hereford and Chichester, and the projected survey of sees 'richly endowed' and ripe for plunder covered only York, Winchester, Durham, Bath, Sarum, Norwich and Worcester. When one considers that Elizabeth's considered opinion of the financial obligations of the episcopate was fundamentally different from that held by Henry VIII both before and after the break from Rome, her approach seems yet more understandable. The obligations of the bishops were considered now to be essentially ecclesiastical. The rigour of the reformers under Edward, and again of the Puritan wing under Elizabeth and the early Stuarts, reinforced this attitude and made it yet more prevalent. Elizabeth disapproved of episcopal marriage and of the need to upkeep episcopal families—she was unlikely to sympathise with such claims from the bishops.

Just how impoverished were the English bishops during the sixteenth century? What economic problems did they have to surmount? What approaches did they use? Until the 1950s it remained impossible to even attempt an answer to such questions as detailed researches into the financial condition of individual bishoprics was all but unattempted; even now, over twenty years later, such studies are in their infancy. Nevertheless it is possible to come to certain tentative conclusions. In studying the finances of the episcopate historians are faced with two major issues —(a) the bishops were now expected to fulfil their own diocesan and domestic obligations and little else, but had depletion of the estates by Crown and courtiers made even this impossible? (b) in an era of inflation were the incomes of the bishops remaining stable or declining in *real* terms? If the answer to this second question is that inflation was seriously affecting the buying power of episcopal money, can the historian find evidence of defences against the effects of inflation?

Research thus far suggests that there is no universally applicable answer to these questions. Dr Cross has demonstrated that at York the money income was maintained at approximately the same level over the period as a whole, although it was derived from a different source in 1600 from that in 1535. She does not comment upon the effects of inflation upon this income and the fact that episcopal demesne in hand was considerably reduced over the period. This last point is of importance because one method whereby the bishops could defend themselves against the worst ravages of inflation was by increasing home production and reducing their dependence upon goods purchased on the open market. Dr Hembry concluded that the diocese of Bath and Wells suffered more than most from the upheavals of the sixteenth century and the depredations of Crown and ministers. She maintained that the later bishops (after the reign of Mary) were under pressure because they had to support families, maintain traditional hospitality, and build up estates for their sons and daughters. She found that the bishops, in consequence, tried to make their estates more remunerative—harrying officials and tenants; converting customary leases into leases for lives; levying fines for lease renewal and heriots mercilessly; supervising markets and fairs; and doubling the productivity of the episcopal lead mines. In her more recent study of Ely Dr Heal has indicated that the diocese suffered less in a real sense from Elizabeth's policy of compulsory land exchanges on unfavourable terms than from earlier confiscations and alienations of property on long leases initiated by the bishops themselves. Dr Heal describes convincingly the manner in which the bishops of Ely were probably able to offset considerably the effects of inflation upon their fairly static money receipts—the see was blessed with such huge reserves of cultivatable land that the bishops were able to provide for their domestic needs to a great extent from their own demesne without the need to purchase supplies at inflated prices.

These sees had something in common initially, for they were all in the wealthy or middling ranges of the list of English and Welsh sees. What happened to the finances of the poorer dioceses during the period 1500–

1642? The case of Coventry and Lichfield is worthy of examination. Prior to 1541 this diocese had included the five archdeaconries of Chester, Coventry, Derby, Salop and Stafford: in 1541 the archdeaconry of Chester was lopped off to form the core of the new diocese of that name. This represented a loss of administrative responsibilities for the see of Coventry and Lichfield and, inevitably, the loss of a certain amount of income potential in terms of fees and so forth, but it should be noted that the see did retain certain estates in Cheshire. From 1537 onwards the see had been forced to part with considerable assets to Crown and courtiers, receiving in exchange somewhat dubious recompense. For instance, when Bishop Sampson relinquished two Staffordshire houses and five valuable manors to the Crown in Henry's reign he received in exchange six rectories, three chapels and a church which were technically worth more than the property surrendered, yet because only one of the rectories was in the diocese itself, the others being in Leicestershire, Northamptonshire and Merionethshire, it was clear that the exchange was to the bishop's disadvantage. It was far more difficult and expensive for him to collect the impropriate tithes; to survey the property and accomplish necessary repairs and improvement and so forth, including the upkeep of chancels and parsonages; and made it easier for others to encroach upon his economic and spiritual rights. In 1547 Sampson also sold some valuable Warwickshire property to the agent of the Duke of Somerset for a nominal rent charge which was eventually remitted altogether.

Calls upon the remaining episcopal revenues were such that there was little or no money available for long-term land improvements which would have eventually increased the productivity of episcopal demesne in hand. Rather, extraordinary demands for money (for instance, for initial payment of first-fruits to the Crown; for occasional payment of subsidies; for immediate payment of debts incurred perhaps by a predecessor) made the bishops acutely aware of their lack of and need for ready money. They were, in consequence, led into policies which were economically short-sighted although effective in raising the necessary immediate sums. The normal recourse of bishops in such circumstances was the leasing of episcopal manors. Until 1559 such transactions customarily involved long leases: for instance, on 19th April 1546, Bishop Sampson leased Farndon, Cheshire, for a term of eighty years. The disadvantages of such a system in the long-term are evident—neither the bishop nor his successors had any prospect of revising the rent due for a lengthy period unless they were able to buy back the lease at considerable expense. As it happened, during a period of galloping inflation the effects of such long leases were most deleterious. The bishops could, and did, exact reasonably high entry fines from the new lessees of episcopal estates. Historians, in the wisdom of hindsight, have seen these high fines as the bishops' way of hedging themselves against the effects of inflated land values and their own inability to raise rents, but in reality the bishops viewed them as an excellent means of securing large amounts of ready cash which were, unlike rents, not subject to Crown tenths, and tenants were willing to pay them because they themselves were secure against regular rent rises. In much the same way tenants were made to finance the improvement of their holdings.

At Coventry and Lichfield successive bishops underwent considerable irritation at the long-leasing policies of their Henrician predecessors, but their approach to the problem in fact made the economic condition of the see worse rather than better. For example, Bishop Baine bought back at least two long leases for an annual payment out of the bishopric; instead of profiting from his transaction by farming the estates himself and improving their yield, he rewarded his relatives and followers with them at the bishopric's expense. The accession of Elizabeth meant that there was considerable uncertainty about the validity of these re-leases (because they had not received confirmation by the Dean and Chapter) [32] and Bishop Bentham, Baine's Protestant successor, spent considerable sums in litigation to recover the properties for the see. This policy of litigation led Bentham into further debt when he was already heavily burdened by the Crown's demands for first-fruits and tenths and subsidy payments, and by his own creditors' requests for payment of sums lent him prior to his entry to the see. The situation at Lichfield might be described as one of cumulative debt.

The Act of 1559 forbade the bishops to make leases for terms longer than 21 years or three lives except to the Crown. The Crown took advantage of this clause on several occasions during Elizabeth's reign, although the terms of rent and fine are unknown [31]. At Lichfield the Elizabethan and Stuart bishops were in an awkward position—like their Henrician, Edwardian and Marian forbears they had need for immediate ready cash but they had no land available for alienation because their predecessors had let it out on long lease. The bishops surmounted this problem in the short term by making immediate reversionary leases (e.g. a lease was granted in 1560 which would not take effect until the present lease came to an end in 1565) or by buying up the current leases and re-leasing on advantageous terms. James I realised that the Act allowing long leases to the Crown was detrimental to episcopal finances and authority and by a self-denying ordinance ended the practice.

Certain of the Stuart bishops of Lichfield exhibited a policy of retrenchment and of husbanding the remaining resources of the see as well as possible. Small increases in rents were achieved under Bishop Morton (1618–1632) and the bishops seem to have attached more importance than ever upon financial rewards from official fees, sale of wood, customary receipts, and so forth [31]. The bishops of Lichfield at no point seem to have concentrated upon increasing the productivity of episcopal demesne. Indeed by the reign of James I little cultivatable land was held in hand and Stuart bishops apparently increased the total revenue of the see not by increasing existing rents significantly but by leasing out as much property as possible and exploiting the other resources of the see. The result was that Morton's secretary reported that the gross receipts of the see (exclusive of a not inconsiderable income from sales of wood, official fees, fees collected at ordinations and institutions, and customary dues) now amounted to £1,114 18s. 5d., which represented a substantial rise over the 1535 figure of £796. Whether this rise in gross receipts compensated for the effects of inflation is doubtful—it certainly could not continue to keep pace with prices as the resources of the episcopate were exploited to their utmost.

This survey of the problems of Coventry and Lichfield cannot tell the whole story. Even an estimate of gross returns from land at various points in time, a measuring of this money income against the effects of inflation—taking into account the possible compensatory effects of home production, and a discussion of the basic approach of various bishops to their immediate financial dilemmas—can take the historian only so far along the road to understanding the true financial predicament of the bishops. Restrictions on all sides limited the possibilities of correcting the situation. Assessed income was not received income, even if the effects of inflation are discounted. Market conditions hemmed in the bishops on all sides. The nature of the episcopal estates—arable, pasture, heath, marsh, woodland—dictated the advantage to which they might be put; their geographical situation determined the degree of effective control the bishop and his officials might exercise over them; the amount of surplus capital affected the scale of farming activities and improvements; the attitude of Crown and Church to excessive exploitation or clearance of episcopal woodland was an effective barrier against the extension of cultivatable land. Moreover, a veritable multitude of side effects must be considered at every stage. Elizabeth's apparently damaging long leases of episcopal property may have resulted in useful remittance of taxation. An increase in money-rents may pale before the knowledge that in reality this increase reflected a depletion of capital assets in kind rather than an exploitation of existing leasing arrangements. Only the acquisition of new property could alleviate the real situation—*in commendam* livings held by Overton, Neile and Morton at Lichfield provided some temporary respite in this respect. The financial position of the bishops has to be assessed not only in the light of money-rents but also of inflation. The study of Coventry and Lichfield, poorer than either Bath and Wells or Ely, suggests that the effects of inflation on money income might vary considerably in importance from see to see. Ely had sufficient cultivatable land after considerable depredation to enable her bishops to weather the storm of inflation; Coventry and Lichfield had never been well endowed in this respect and there came a point during the sixteenth century when the exploitation of the home farm as a hedge against inflation was no longer a viable possibility and further alienation of endowed land by lease was inevitable.

Dr Christopher Haigh's discussion of the financial problems of the diocese of Chester has underlined several of the specific difficulties of the new dioceses. There was a tremendous financial advantage to the Crown in combining low revenues with the largest possible administrative area, using existing jurisdictional boundaries. Chester was next to Rochester the poorest of the English sees in 1535 and the fourth poorest in 1575. Her revenue was drawn from spiritualities (appropriated rectories for the most part) rather than from temporalities: whereas most of the revenue of the old sees was drawn from land (only 10 per cent being derived from 'spiritualities' in 1535) two-thirds of Chester's income was drawn from spiritualities and she held only one manor. After 1547 none of her income was from land. This placed the bishop in a quandary: he had only one episcopal residence, which made travel in his diocese difficult; his opportunities for the exploitation of his property were severely limited—he had no demesne for production of food, no woods, no profits from manorial rights. Dr Haigh suggests that in the interests of financial solvency (particularly during a period of rapid inflation) the bishops of Chester sacrificed the efficient administration and pastoral care of their large diocese.

The view of Elizabeth's attitude to church plunder has to be revised again slightly: it is true that she seems to have stolen directly only from the rich and to have left the poor alone; it is true that in the early years of her reign she granted certain concessions to the poorer bishops—Bentham of Coventry and Lichfield, for example, seems to have been released (after much pleading) from payment of at least part of his first-fruits; however, the recent research on a poorer diocese suggests that such were finding it difficult to meet even minimal obligations without diminishing episcopal resources still further and that the Crown should have been augmenting the revenues of the poorer sees, not simply leaving them alone.

During the sixteenth century Crown and courtiers had joined in plunder of the Church—men had grown accustomed to ask to what use church wealth was being put. The attack upon church wealth was reinforced by the views of the Puritan wing of the Church. Even at the end of Elizabeth's reign many bishops still lived in feudal splendour (even if they found difficulty in paying for it) and the Puritans recommended further rape of episcopal wealth. The bishops, however, were a part of the traditional landlord class. Their chief difference from the remainder of this class was that they, like the Crown, could not sell their freehold outright. Landlords may have despised the bishops because of their increasingly middle-class/lower-class origins but they were much frightened by this Puritan attack on the traditional order. The Crown, similarly, realised that the usefulness of the Church as propagandist pillar of the monarchy depended upon the maintenance of its economic position.

The seventeenth century, therefore, witnessed a conservative alliance to maintain the economic strength of the episcopate against the attacks of Puritan laymen and ecclesiastics. James I stopped the practice of taking long leases on church property. His son, under the influence of Archbishop Laud, in 1633 abolished the practice of the leasing of episcopal land for lives—henceforth the bishops could lease only on terms of 21 years or less. A survey was ordered of all bishops' and dean and chapter lands: the results would give the parties concerned a chance to raise fines and rents at shorter intervals and thereby also increase gentry and yeoman dependence upon their ecclesiastical landlords as they would have to apply for new leases more frequently. The 1629 Royal Instructions which ordered bishops to live in their sees in episcopal houses, unless their presence was requested at court, would also have had the effect of making the bishop's presence felt locally and could have affected episcopal control of estate management. In 1634 royal attention was turned directly towards control of plunder of resources by the bishops themselves. The Bishop of Bristol was ordered to hold a certain manor in hand or, if he leased it, to lease it for the term of his own episcopate only. The government supervised episcopal activities regarding releasing of property. Bishops' raping of timber supplies was controlled: the Bishop of Winchester, for example, was forbidden to bind himself to provide wood for the repair of tenants' houses in an effort to conserve supplies; the Bishop of Coventry and Lichfield was charged with exploiting the episcopal woods. Archbishop Laud discussed with the Dean and Chapter of Winchester the possibility of annulling the ancient copyhold customs in favour of more advantageous leasehold policies. When the Dean and Chapter extracted heavy entry fines on Chapter property, they were made to use them to finance cathedral repairs. When certain *in commendam* livings were annexed permanently to the poorer bishoprics, Laud demanded that account be made for them on a regular basis to ensure that the bishops concerned were not leasing out the same.

That this was a sensible policy cannot be denied, but Laud could not make it thorough-going because of opposition from both within and without the Church. Laudian policy involved an attempt not only to increase episcopal resources but also to improve clerical incomes as a whole. He hoped to resume for this purpose lay impropriations of clerical livings and tithes. Over the country as a whole, five-sixths of the benefices in 1604 were controlled by laymen in respect of impropriate tenths (tithes), leasing of tithes, and/or patronage. In many impropriate rectories the lay rector partook of most of the tithes of the parish and awarded the clerical vicar but a small share of this wealth as an augmentation; in many parishes no augmentation whatsoever was offered. The situation was abhorrent but an attack upon impropriations amounted to an attack on a very important property right, which landowners would not tolerate. Crown, nobility, gentry (including parliamentarians and many Puritan laymen), and ecclesiastics all had a vested interest in impropriations. During the 1630s Laud was greatly influenced by Bishop Morton of Durham who saw the resumption of impropriations as a means of augmenting poor vicarages. In 1634 a test case was won whereby it was ruled that the Church had the right to compel impropriators to augment vicarages in their parishes. In 1635 Laud ordered Bishop Williams of Lincoln to ensure augmentation of poor vicarages on this basis. The Privy Council, working on the basis of petitions from poor vicars, ordered a considerable number of such augmentations. Yet, the results of this campaign were very insignificant prior to 1640. The actual resumption of impropriations was a dismal failure—the Crown did not declare a policy of surrendering impropriations to the Church until 1646 when the possibility of actually accomplishing the act was remote. Detailed schemes were evolved for the buying in of impropriations by means of general subscription throughout Charles I's reign but these never succeeded because of lay opposition. If Whitgift was correct in estimating that the annual loss to the church of England through impropriations amounted to £100,000, it is clear that a plan was confounded which would have righted the perilous economic position of many of the parish clergy at one blow and would have removed pressure from the only other available source for augmentation—episcopal and dean and chapter lands.

There is no doubt that Christopher Hill is correct when he says that Laud was trying to set the clock back a hundred years in pursuing this policy—instead of utilising the prejudices of the landowners and the Puritans he was swimming against the tide of their vested interests. The old ruling class wanted to continue to exploit the Church through patronage, impropriations and leases of tithes—they saw no reason why the episcopal estates should not be treated as cavalierly as those of the monks before them and this predilection for plunder was reinforced by a view that the religious justification for feudal bishops was dubious. The political rule of bishops was anathema to these men—they had no sympathy with the desire of Charles I and Laud to use the bishops as a bolster for monarchical power. The new men—the improving landlords and the few industrialists—found that the bishops obstructed advances already and recoiled from Laudian projects for the tithing of industrial production. The yeomen and husbandmen suffered in a very immediate way at the hands of the episcopate and the impecunious, litigious clergy. Religious Puritanism seems to have organised these inherent economic objections to the economic revival of the Church at both diocesan and parochial level.

The economic position of the Church in 1642 was very different from that it occupied in 1539. At the dissolution approximately one-quarter of the nation's landed wealth had been redistributed, to Crown and laymen. Even if the Crown's plunder of the episcopate especially after 1558 has been overstressed by historians, the monarchy and certain courtiers had profited from exchanges with the bishops. The control of the regular orders over the parishes of England (in terms of both patronage and tithes) had passed into the hands of laymen. The bishops had relatively little control over the appointment and payment of their own parochial clergy. The laity who were in control were fundamentally unsympathetic to the aspirations (or indeed the very existence) of the Anglican bishops. Although technically the bishops were still great landlords and important to the nation's economy, few of them were holding large quantities of land in hand and engaging in farming activity. They formed part of a *rentier* landlord class and only occasionally can evidence of their improving farming activities be discovered. They tended to be most preoccupied with their own financial survival, and with maintaining friendly relations with the local gentry by granting favourable leases, rather than with the improvement of the resources of the see. The relative decline in the importance of ecclesiastical landed wealth in the economy was heightened by the increase in importance of improving lay landlords and of the emergence of non-landed sectors of society into economic prominence.

Historians have not tackled in detail the problem of the English episcopate in the post-Restoration period. In 1660 many of the Laudians captured key positions in the Church but they were not able to push through any sort of reforming programme because of the abolition of High Commission and other prerogative courts; moreover, there was no longer a close connection with the government as there had been before 1640. Christopher Hill believes that although there were no more attempts to raise tithe payments, recover secularised property, or enforce a clerical social programme, many of the economic problems of the Church were solved incidentally by the great agricultural prosperity which England experienced during the late seventeenth and eighteenth centuries and also by the direct attack on such problems enshrined in Queen Anne's Bounty. The extent to which he is justified in making this claim must remain uncertain until historians have studied in depth the economic position of the Church during this period.

# 7

# The Importance of Foreign Trade

The chapters in this book have been concerned in the main with the internal affairs of England and Wales, but no collection of studies of the social and economic history of early modern England would be complete without some consideration of her foreign trade. Historians have always followed contemporaries in according international trade a place of high importance in their accounts. As has been indicated, the economy of early modern England was still predominantly agricultural, so why was foreign trade deemed so important?

Governments throughout the period were anxious to encourage foreign trade in English ships, especially in time of peace, as a means of maintaining the country's fleet and continuing the art of navigation. In war-time the country drew its vessels from among the merchant ships and its core of fighting sailors from amongst the merchant crews. The standing fleet itself was small and ill-manned during peace-time. The principle upon which the system operated was closely akin to that relating to the armed forces, which were drawn predominantly from the local trained bands produced by the musters. The technical problems posed in relation to the fleet were more numerous, however. The requisitioned merchant ships upon which the navy relied in war-time completely until the time of Oliver Cromwell's protectorate, and to some degree during the Protectorate and the Restoration periods, had to be of a suitable build to stand up to the rigours of warfare. A bounty was offered to encourage the building of ships of over 100 tons. It was only the more distant trading companies which employed really large ships (of up to 400 tons or more) but because the trade was distant there was a real disadvantage in that the ships were rarely in port and available for use. All merchants argued that their commerce supported navigation. The East India Company's ships were the most suitable, if rarely available; the Eastland and Levant companies employed adequate vessels which were in port several times a year. Although the boats used in the coastal coal trade were useless as warships, the merchants involved in the trade argued that they acted as veritable nurseries of seamen. Whereas the merchant companies argued that they employed the better ships, the free trading merchants stressed that they owned more ships which served an invaluable supportive function in time of war. Throughout the period the government encountered a major problem in that English importers and exporters showed a distinct preference for using Dutch or Baltic freighters to carry their bulky goods, largely because English carrying ships were expensive—the consequence was that few native ships of the necessary tonnage were being constructed. Successive Navigation Acts attempted to reverse this situation. The Great Navigation Act of 1540, for example, served to encourage the English carrying trade, and indirectly the building of suitable ships, by excluding exports in foreign vessels from its benefits. During the reign of James I, the monarch's conciliatory attitude towards the Dutch forbade attempts to impose a Navigation Act, and at a time when English trade was suffering heavily as a consequence of the thriving Dutch carrying trade, it was small wonder that in 1634 Charles I attempted to collect ship-money from inland areas in order to finance the building of a new fleet. There can be little doubt that it was awareness of the inadequacy of the merchant ships available which led the Long Parliament to build from scratch an efficient standing navy. Nevertheless, one of the guidelines of Cromwellian and later Stuart commercial policy was still to encourage trading ventures which might strengthen the merchant fleet, simply because it was still an important supplementary force. Moreover, shortage of money meant that the government could not build as many new ships as were necessary. Whereas 147 warships were built between 1649 and 1654, only 60 were built during the Protectorate. If the Navigation Acts were designed in part to encourage native shipping, this does not mean that they were popular with the merchant seamen—on the contrary, most English exporters found the rules against using Dutch carrying ships irksome and, in that they provoked Dutch reprisals, directly harmful to their export trade. The fishermen of Yarmouth found that their soaring trade in pickled herrings was much damaged, and protested so vigorously that in 1657 the section of the Act of 1651 directly related to their trade was repealed. Moreover, there is every reason to doubt that the Navigation Acts did result in the building of more suitable ships. The Act of 1660 forbade English importers the use of foreign ships to carry goods from the Baltic. The English merchants involved did not have ships of the necessary tonnage to carry timber imports and the direct effect of the clause seems to have been to drive English merchants from the Baltic trade. Of course, the Navigation Acts can be seen to have redirected English trade from the old markets to new colonial ones but there is room for doubt that they actually served to increase the volume of English controlled trade.

Agrarian economy though hers was, a surprising number of England's inhabitants were, either directly or indirectly, dependent upon the sea and foreign trade for their livelihood. The government, continually pre-occupied with the problems of unemployment and vagrancy and incipient rebellion, were concerned with the encouragement of foreign trade for this reason also. It would be easy to make a list of occupations which were in some respect reliant upon the continuance of trade—not only those actually involved in the building, supplying or manning of ships and ports but almost everyone concerned in industrial production. Professor Ralph Davis has suggested that one-quarter of the total industrial product of England at the end of the seventeenth century was destined for export, and that this picture was generally representative of the preceding two centuries. The nature of trade had to be carefully regulated in order to enhance rather than destroy the occupational opportunities at home. For instance, the importer who imported dressed flax was doing a disservice—he was removing employment from the hands of the flax-dressers of the Home Counties. The dependence of industrial concerns upon foreign trade is demonstrably true in the case of the cloth trade which followed two broad patterns in the sixteenth century—some craftsmen merely worked to satisfy the needs of their local communities, never looking to inter-regional, let alone international, markets; but there existed also a few highly-organised specialist producers, supervised by merchants, who did work for the export market. By 1700 approximately one-half of the woollen cloth produced was exported overseas. It was this organised sector of the woollen cloth trade which had shown the most marked expansion in the later sixteenth and seventeenth centuries, due to increased demand from foreign rather than home markets. Merchants organised the industry around the putting-out system, which permitted the necessary division of labour to fulfil specialist functions. Throughout Europe it was the textile manufacturing industries which engaged most actively in international commerce, albeit often over short distances. Towards the end of the seventeenth century England exported more and more metal and leather products, and export of grain became increasingly significant but, for the most part, there was only truly significant export of textiles. For this reason depressions in foreign trade showed themselves most acutely among the cloth-workers. When the boom in export of the 'old draperies' collapsed in 1614 the slump hit the West Country hard, but this was followed by a yet more severe crisis in the early 1620s when local JPs in the west and in Suffolk reported that they feared mutiny—the situation was compounded by the coincidence of a bad harvest and high food prices in 1621, and as Professor B. E. Supple has said 1622 saw the bottom of the economic trough, with immense unemployment in Gloucestershire, Wiltshire, Oxfordshire, Exeter, and London amongst other places. In Wiltshire 8,000 were unemployed. London cloth-workers were forced to emigrate. Depression hit again in 1625 and 1629 and, according to the most recent historian of Somerset, distress was general and acute amongst the cloth-workers of the whole region around Frome and Shepton Mallet for some twenty years before the outbreak of the Civil War. The total cloth trade of England itself may have been revolutionised and redirected, in the form of the 'new draperies' into fresh markets but this did not alter the extent of the social and economic dislocation caused by the collapse of the 'old draperies' in the west [33].

Naturally enough governments sought to encourage the foreign trade through England's ports, both import and export, in order to mulct it for additional revenue. The ports defined a frontier which it was possible to regulate, and because Customs rose as trade increased they were to an extent inflation-proof. Of course, the Crown had, with varying success, to strike a balance between tariffs favourable enough to encourage traffic yet high enough to yield sufficient profit. (As will be indicated later, a conflict of interests between the merchants themselves and the State, and between different theories of economic policy were ever present in this aspect of foreign trade.) By the late sixteenth century the Customs accounted for one-third of the Crown's revenue; by 1611 the proportion had risen to a half of the total royal revenue. Until the mid-sixteenth century the Crown had lost considerably financially by the fact that Customs impositions were low on cloth and higher on raw wool exports whereas the great expansion in the export trade had been in woollen cloth after the failure of the wool export trade in 1521. In 1558 Mary altered the situation by imposing a higher duty on cloth. Other exported commodities were rated at so much in the pound of their estimated value according to the book of rates. Unfortunately for the Crown such official ratings were made very infrequently and so the revenue from Customs was liable to lag behind the rate of inflation: the rate was in reality not normally higher than five pence in the pound. The Crown also met with severe difficulties in the collection of duties—smuggling, corruption amongst Customs officials, and inefficient collection at some of the outports, had an incalculable effect upon total receipts. By 1604 the government had set up the Great Farm of the Customs. Initially this was granted to three businessmen for a term of seven years—the yield of the Great Farm was £112,000 per annum. By this means, the government ensured a fixed income which was immune to the occasionally catastrophic effects of trading slumps and foreign embargoes (for example in 1560–3 the yield was 40 per cent lower than in 1558–60); moreover, the arrangement was short-term and therefore it could be revised in the light of current conditions when it terminated. In actual fact, the rental was raised during the course of the initial term, so that by 1614 the farm was yielding £140,000. Of course, the farmers made a profit out of the Customs but the Crown was grateful for the opportunity of a guaranteed income and also for the possibilities of obtaining outright loans and anticipations of future rentals from the syndicate farmers who were controlling the Customs in the 1630s. The Customs revenue was so important to the Stuarts that at various times they tried to exercise ever greater control over it. In Bate's case in 1606 judgement was given in favour of the King's right to impose duties without parliamentary approval for the purposes of regulating trade. In fact there were but a few non-parliamentary duties—those on currants and tobacco being best-known—but the principle was an important one. Oliver Cromwell triumphed in a similar battle—Cony's case—in 1654 when his right to levy Customs by mere ordinance was confirmed. The government attempted to raise the yield of the Customs but they remained in farm until 1671 when they were taken over and administered by commissioners.

As Dr Maurice Ashley has shown, the actual yield of the Customs was very closely associated with trading figures. The English figures for Customs receipts showed a considerable rise in the years 1653–4 (£328,317; £364,486 as opposed to £250,863 in 1651 and £266,070 in 1652) as compared with the Dutch which were at their all-time low of the century during those years and were lower than the English receipts. Dr Ashley attributes this situation to England's general economic recovery at the close of the First Dutch War and to the fact that England was apparently gaining trade at the expense of the Dutch. Yet after the conclusion of a peace in April 1654 the two countries Customs receipts followed a like path until 1660 when they diverged sharply—the Dutch rose from 1,757,182 gilders to 2,048,254 (at a rate of £1=11 gilders) while the English fell from £482,820 to £285,000—which points to the conclusion that the Dutch profited from the dislocation caused by the Restoration. He also suggests that a temporary fall in English receipts from Easter 1657 is attributable to the active prosecution of the Spanish War, whose termination in 1659 accounts for the revival of trade and the Customs revenues. The Restoration Parliament of 1660 voted Customs duties according to a new book of rates which promised to yield some £400,000 a year. Because of difficulties in enforcing payment, Customs officials were empowered to break into suspected houses and by 1662 to search ships both inward and outward bound and to seize and store 'smuggled' goods until duties were paid. Despite the favourable rating and these precautions, the yield of the Customs averaged barely £300,000 for the first four years of Charles II's reign and fell off during the course of the two Dutch wars because of the interruptions to trade. 1674 saw the beginning of an improvement and by the late 1680s when trade was at its peak the Customs yield amounted to £640,000. Clearly, at a time when the combined revenue from Customs and Excise amounted to between two-thirds and three-quarters of total government revenue, the Crown had every reason to foster the growth of foreign trade.

Indirectly also, the wealth of the merchant community was of considerable interest to the Crown, which was always seeking for possible sources of loans. The Company of Merchant Adventurers and the City of London raised money from the merchant community to lend to the Crown. Even with the emergence of more sophisticated borrowing facilities, it remained true that merchant investment in the Bank of England was high.

There was also a common belief that foreign trade increased a nation's international prestige and power. In a nation's trade lay her wealth. A country which was prosperous was perforce respected. Moreover, the government could employ trading regulations to inhibit the opportunities of rivals, to favour the trade of allies, or to encourage the expansion of its own international trade along specified, desirable lines. Advantage in foreign trade might skilfully be employed as an advantage in international diplomacy. The Englishman Thomas Mun put it well when he said: 'Behold then the true form and worth of foreign trade, which is the great revenue of the king, the honour of the kingdom, the noble profession of the merchant, the school of our arts, the supply of our wants, the employment of our poor, the improvement of our lands, the nursery of our mariners, the walls of the kingdom, the means of our treasure, the sinews of our wars, the terror of our enemies.' (*England's Treasure by Forraign Trade*, 1664).

The economic crises of the sixteenth and seventeenth centuries inspired many politicians and merchants to attempt remedies both for particular, immediate maladies and for the state of English trade in general. Although the term Mercantilism is normally employed by historians to describe economic policies broached in the late seventeenth and eighteenth centuries, there can be little doubt that many were advocating what were essentially mercantilist lines of action from the early sixteenth century onwards. Foreign trade was important partly because England had to pay for rapidly increasing foreign imports; it was felt to be undesirable to pay for these in specie, far better to do so in kind—fundamentally, foreign trade was conceived of as an 'exchange'. Sixteenth-century pre-occupation with the 'terms of trade' arose from a desire to see that England did not suffer in this exchange of goods. Out of this grew an increasing feeling that England should not only seek the most favourable terms of trade but also strive to achieve a balance of trade in which exports far exceeded in value that of imported goods. In this way it was hoped that England would draw in from foreign countries bullion as payment for exports, thus actually increasing her wealth by foreign trade and, moreover, increasing the amount of money in circulation. At the same time, England would strive to be more self-sufficient, husbanding her resources, utilising raw materials grown or mined at home, and certainly not contributing them to the store of another nation. This view envisaged trade as a 'battle' in which the nation strove to be as independent of other 'powers' as possible, and to render these same powers as dependent upon her own trade as she could. The government, long accustomed to intervene in order to foster foreign trade and regulate it for purposes of defence, would be called upon to regulate trade, both exports and imports, in order to allow the above system to operate. There is no doubt that this opinion was lent a far sharper edge by trading and political rivalry with the Dutch in the seventeenth century and, traditionally, its formulation as an economic doctrine is attributed to Thomas Mun as late as 1621, yet Francis Bacon was a convinced mercantilist before this, and sixteenth-century reformers and governments voiced similar opinions. Thus the author of *The Discourse of the Common Weal of this Realm of England* in 1549 urged that 'we must alwaies take care that we bie no more of strangers than we sell them . . . for so wee sholde empoverishe owr selves and enriche them'. Such a favourable balance of trade would lead to a much needed influx of bullion—necessary because coin was light, unperishable, internationally valid, and easily divided into smaller denominations. This was the core dogma of later mercantilism.

The depression in the cloth trade also inspired many similar views. After 1521 Britain's once great export of wool became insignificant and the trade in semi-finished cloth took over the former importance of raw wool. In the 1530s there were complaints that full advantage was not being taken of Britain's trading opportunities in this respect. In the mid-decade the pamphleteer Clement Armstrong considered that the Calais staple was not doing its job properly because it was distributing raw wool to be manufactured by foreign competitors, and this even at rock-bottom prices and with little or no attempt to stimulate increased production of English wool. Armstrong's remedy lay in an insistence by the government upon the home manufacture and finishing of woollen cloth. He allowed that there should be some export of the raw material but suggested that this should be controlled by the King who could fix the price and thus increase his yield from the Customs. As Professor Geoffrey Elton points out, Armstrong, who lacked Thomas Cromwell's mercantile experience, failed to appreciate that there would be no market in the Netherlands for finished cloth, as this would bring ruin to the Brabant finishing industry.

Although the Reformation parliament saw one bill designed to forbid the export of unfinished cloth and two more hostile to the Merchant Adventurers, Cromwell himself never seriously intended to ban such exports because of his understanding of trade conditions. Instead he tried to encourage existing exports. The Great Navigation Act of 1540 served to encourage the English carrying trade by excluding exports in foreign vessels from its benefits although the effects of this measure were soon eroded. Cromwell did seek to enforce one other maxim of the mercantilists. In 1533 an Act was passed to encourage the growing of flax and hemp, with the stated motive of creating a linen and rope industry and of stopping unnecessary import of such goods. Cromwell was so attached to this scheme that in 1536 he repealed a monopoly by which the Linendrapers closely regulated and restricted production of linen. A similar attempt to import a silk industry was made. In 1538 Cromwell intervened at the request of Sir Richard Gresham to free the foreign exchange. The 1530s saw the government extremely concerned at the drainage of coin from England; a commission of 1531 led by Thomas More recommended complete stoppage of the exchequer which would permit no export of specie either in the form of cash or bills of exchange; an Act of 1536 unsuccessfully attempted to enforce such a stoppage but by 1537 a licensing system was in operation; however, by 1538 the detrimental effects of the stoppage on trade were clearly visible and a repeal was effected—it was accepted that free exchange was essential if trade were to flourish.

It was a depression in the cloth trade of the 'old draperies' which fathered one of the best-known and ill-fated of merchant industrial projects of the seventeenth century—Cockayne's project. England's trade in heavy undyed broadcloths from the West Midlands and East Anglia had been booming, despite the slump in 1610 and some forebodings in 1613, until over 127,000 cloths were exported in 1614. There was much feeling, however, that England was not prospering as she might from her cloth exports—technological weakness compelled her to leave the profitable finishing processes on the cloth to others: perhaps as much as 75 per cent of the profit stemming from cloth manufacture was going to the Dutch. The Merchant Adventurers Company, which had usurped the position of the Hanse merchants as England's leading exporters of cloth, still flourished because it sold unfinished cloth to a ready market in Holland. The Eastland Company, which exported finished and dyed cloths to the Baltic states, found that they were being undercut pricewise in the Baltic by Dutch merchants who masqueraded English cloths finished in Holland as Dutch and tried to put English products in a bad light by advertising their faulty cloth lengths ostentatiously as 'English'.

Alderman Cockayne of London, a member of the Eastland company and one of the King's creditors, put forward a plausible scheme to the King designed to defeat Dutch competition and to promote England's own economic development. Briefly, the project consisted of the King revoking the Merchant Adventurers' exclusive right to export undyed cloths to Holland (which was done in December 1614), and of replacing the old system of exporting semi-finished products by one which placed the entire manufacturing and retailing process in English hands. Although the project found most support in the Eastland Company, members of the Levant Company and the cloth-workers and dyers of London were all in its favour. The King, moreover, found the prospect of a further £40,000 in revenue from Customs on dye-stuffs and on the exports alluring and could not resist complying with Cockayne's wishes. Although the reasoning behind the project was plausible, it was from the first unlikely that the English could learn the secrets pertaining to the finishing and dyeing process sufficiently quickly to make the plan work: it was basically because of this lack of the necessary manpower and skills that the project collapsed. Moreover, the state of the market was already depressed and production of cloth of the right kind was at a low ebb—more and more wool was being put into developing the so-called 'new draperies' for a southern European market. Even had the project succeeded in producing sufficient cloth of the required quality and finish, it would have found no market. A Dutch *Plakaat* forbade importation, sale, or weaving of cloth manufactured and dyed in Britain; at the same time incentives were offered to encourage the growth of the Dutch cloth-weaving industry. For the next two decades the English government and merchants dedicated themselves to achieving the restoration of the *status quo* as regards this particular market. The major trade depressions of 1622, 1630, and 1649–50, however, all saw a revival of

Cockayne's fundamental idea—that trading rivals should be denied access to England's raw materials and that England herself should expand industrial production to maximise her natural advantages.

It is to the thought of Thomas Mun, expressed in evidence given to the Commissioners of Trade in 1662, that one looks for the classic mercantilist remedy to England's ills. As Professor Wilson commented, Mun formulated his doctrines in opposition to those who held that England's economic crisis was due to a loss of treasure and coin through the undervaluing of English money in exchange and who saw a remedy either in the imposition of exchange controls or in the raising of the nominal value of the silver coinage. Mun, on the other hand, believed that the problem lay in the flow of trade—a favourable balance of trade was essential for recovery. He reiterated the thoughts expressed earlier in 1549: 'The ordinary means therefore to encrease our wealth and treasure is by Forraign Trade, wherein wee must ever observe this rule; to sell more to strangers yearly than wee consume of theirs in value.' Wealth, in the form of goods or bullion, would be drawn into the kingdom either by an expansion of exports or by a reduction of imports or by a combination of both methods. The policy Mun advocated implied economic warfare with the Dutch: the Dutch were exploiting England's natural advantages—the fisheries, the wool industry, the carrying trade —which England must hasten to exploit for herself. When luxurious living relied upon excessive importation, then it must be curtailed. He also had some warning against the excessive dependence of English trade and manufacture upon the fortunes of the cloth trade—he advocated as compensation an expansion of tillage and fishing. He employed the weapons given him by the theorist who defended England's rights to her fishing grounds—notably John Selden's *Mare Liberum*—to attack the Dutch for founding their economic strength upon the resources of another nation 'like a fair bird suited with goodly borrowed plumes'.

Was his analysis of England's economic malaise correct? Until fairly recently many historians believed that the dislocating effect of Cockayne's project was to a large extent responsible for the decay of the cloth trade in the 1620s. However, in the 1950s this view was challenged, although even now no historian would deny that Cockayne's scheme aggravated the market and provoked the Dutch. Some have suggested that the start of the Thirty Years War in 1618 caused serious disruption of trade; others that English cloth was being priced out of the market for one reason or another. Dr J. D. Gould tested several of these theories. Although contemporaries noticed some dislocation of trade by the continental wars they did not lay great stress upon this and indeed also commented that the war had actually brought some advantages in the form of fresh markets. Far more common was the complaint that English cloth was too dear to be profitable. It was claimed that various impositions such as Customs, licensing fees, consumption money and various foreign fees made a Worcester broadcloth (high quality) cost £4 13s. more than a Dutch cloth.

But was this really the cause of the slump? Most of the English Customs and the imposed foreign duties had been in force long before the trade decayed; this applied also to licence fees and consumption money. Even more pertinent is the fact that trade revived without the removal of any of these impositions. Also, trade figures show that the major decline in cloth exports and sales occurred in the Baltic and not in the Low Countries where the most onerous duties were levied [34].

Dr Gould, while not denying that the protectionist policies of the Dutch seriously damaged England's trade in broadcloths at this time, nevertheless sought the true explanation for the expensiveness of English cloth in the price revolution. This movement affected different countries at different times. During the late sixteenth century although English prices rose markedly they did so less rapidly than on the Continent: because of this England's export trade enjoyed a competitive advantage. The reign of James I, however, witnessed a change in the situation—English prices rose very markedly while they tended to stabilize on the Continent or even to fall. For example, the whole of the first half of the seventeenth century saw price stability in the United Provinces, and in Danzig, where English trade in cloth was very active, prices fell throughout these years. The English traders were now at a disadvantage in that their goods were more expensive than those of their competitors. Nevertheless, this situation was a long-term one and while it illustrates the susceptibility of the export market to general price rises in the long run, it does not offer an explanation for the slump of the 1620s in particular.

A more specific explanation may be discovered in the developments within the Baltic trade. Firstly, whereas the English normally strove to balance their exports with imports, and to sell their surplus exports for money, there were severe obstacles to this course in the 1620s. The Baltic merchants were loath to purchase English goods with coin; the bulk of the import trade to England was being undertaken by Dutch ships (timber and iron) and the normal importing undertaken by the English was curtailed—because England had experienced a succession of good harvests, there was little or no reason to import grain from the Baltic. The merchants in this area stood to suffer a loss in their exporting if they could not obtain in return either specie or goods. The problem was accentuated by the very limited use of the bill of exchange in the Baltic area. Secondly, the Thirty Years War brought in its wake serious currency and exchange instability—both the Eastland and the Merchant Adventurers Companies bore witness to the fact that the coinage in both the Baltic and Germany was seriously debased. This inevitably caused a sharp depreciation in exchange rates in those areas, which was not countered by a like price rise: because of this the export trade suffered. Dr Gould sees this as the major cause of the trade crisis of the 1620s, firstly because there is a close chronological correlation between the debasements and the onset of the cloth trade crisis in the Baltic and, secondly, because the trade recovery noted in 1623–4 coincided with successful attempts by the Baltic powers to put their currencies on a sure footing once more.

This analysis suggests that contemporaries such as Mun were incorrect in blaming the onset of depression on to Dutch trade rivalry and on to the failure of the British Crown to protect its own trade, choosing as it did to sacrifice the general interest to the vested interests of the companies. Yet at the same time the question of the effect of the prevailing rate of exchange upon the outflow of specie was being hotly contested. There were those like Malynes who believed that a too-low rate of exchange was independently encouraging imports and the efflux of bullion and advocated direct control of the rates to the permanent trade commissioners in 1623; and there were those who followed Mun in maintaining that the exchange rates would rise naturally from an increase in exports against imports—the undervaluation recommended by Malynes in 1623 'which these men call the abuse of the exchange, . . . is in truth nothing else but the declination of our trade which vents not half so many cloths and yet spends twice as much lawns, cambrics and the like as in times past'.

Certainly, concentration upon the Dutch threat was natural in the circumstances because the Dutch were succeeding where England was failing and, moreover, the English were becoming increasingly dependent upon Amsterdam for both their import and export trades [35]. It was possible to purchase foreign luxury merchandise at a cheaper price from the Amsterdam entrepôt than from the country of origin—this attracted English importers to Amsterdam and benefited Dutch trade and Dutch shipping [36]. Moreover, those English traders who sailed direct to the countries concerned, tried to compete with the Dutch entrepôt by cutting sailing costs—they did this by using cheap Dutch transport, leading in its turn to the decay of English navigation and to the profit of the Dutch. The English balance of payments suffered because the services of the Dutch shipowners were paid for in coin. In the export trade also the Dutch were rivals for the profit from English trade—they triumphed as regards the dyeing and finishing of cloth. When in the early 1620s the English cloth trade was catastrophically affected by falling exchange rates in the Baltic and Germany, the Dutch stood to profit at their expense, taking more and more unfinished English cloth at advantageous rates. Small wonder that the English resented Dutch rivalry and demanded government action to reverse the trend.

With regard to the governmental attitude to such merchant demands throughout the seventeenth century, several points deserve special mention. Firstly, and obviously, the English Crown was guided in its commercial policy by other considerations than the advance of foreign trade—internal political considerations and the interests of international diplomacy were very important. The merchants belonging to the trading companies wanted to defeat the Dutch entrepôt but James I defeated attempts to pass a Navigation Act. His personal policy was one of conciliation towards the Dutch; he foresaw considerable administrative difficulties in enforcing such an Act; he preferred to offer protection to specific trades and avoid outright confrontation with the Low Countries. His son, Charles I, was hamstrung in his commercial relations with the United Provinces by the family connection with the House of Orange: his daughter Mary was married to William of Orange. Moreover, a free trade lobby, which opposed regulation of trade via merchant trading companies, had some influence during the 1620s and actually succeeded in having the Merchant Adventurers Company opened up to free traders during the Parliament of 1621.

The entire calamitous reign of Charles I can be viewed as an example of a government seeking political viability via a conciliatory policy towards overseas merchants and financiers. The years 1625–9 witnessed Charles's attempt to govern with the consent of the landed interest but the dissolution of Parliament in 1629 may be seen as marking his decision to attempt to rule with the help of the big commercial interests rather than land. As Professor Hugh Kearney wrote 'from now on the merchant oligarchies controlling the Levant Company and the East India Company began to enjoy political influence commensurate with their great wealth'. Foreign policy was made in accordance with the larger commercial interests—Weston, Cottington, Laud and Wentworth all supported the peace negotiations and peace treaties with France and Spain. Later in 1637 Wentworth doubted that 'war tends in any sort to the wealth or safety of the Crown of England' but 'rather to the decay of trade', arguing that while France and Spain warred with one another it was English trade which profited from their involvement, to the great improvement of the Customs receipts and English navigation. Peace with Spain seemed essential in view of the fact that an expanding market for the 'new draperies' had been found in southern Spain which compensated for the decay of the trade in the 'old draperies' in the Baltic. Such a policy found especial support in the Levant and East India Companies who stood for profit, rather than in the Merchant Adventurers which was still heavily engaged in the old trade. The companies tended to view the Netherlands not as a fellow Protestant country but as a serious trading rival—their enthusiasms in this respect were only curbed by Charles I's own peculiarly strong family loyalties. The decision to levy ship-money itself was taken against a background of commerce and foreign policy rather than domestic politics: a strong fleet was felt to be desirable to protect English shipping against piracy in the Mediterranean, as well as in the Channel. The merchant financiers raised no opposition to the extension of the levy to the inland counties.

Charles's downfall was that he never possessed the confidence of a large part of the commercial world which he was trying so hard to woo. He always relied upon support from the great financiers and the larger monopolistic merchant companies but his policies served to alienate the lesser merchants and 'interlopers' and men who were investing in trade in a small way [37]. Many felt that the government's commercial foreign policy sacrificed the interests of the small men while protecting the Levant and East India Companies: peace with Spain, for instance, meant that merchants seeking to colonise parts of the Lesser Antilles were open to Spanish attack. The fact that many of the men engaged in such enterprises, particularly the joint-stock Providence company, were fervent Puritans tended to combine them into a commercial religious lobby which opposed trade war against the Dutch, urging instead hostilities against Catholic Spain, and demanded government attention to the possibilities and problems of New World colonisation. Laud's religious policy combined to alienate the Puritan merchants and entrepreneurs still further; practically all the government's other schemes were made unpalatable as Laudianism became equated with Caroline policy.

The course of trade itself had checkered the fortunes of the free trade lobby presented by outport merchants and interlopers since James I's reign. The lobby, supported in Parliament, had seen limited success when trade with France, Spain and Portugal was opened up to merchants outside the companies in 1606. But a trade boom took much of the force from the free traders' argument against the monopolistic companies. As we have seen, the depression of 1621 awoke the campaign anew—the Parliament of that year saw a vigorous parliamentary attack upon three major companies (Merchant Adventurers; East India; and Muscovy). It was this group which attributed the depression in the cloth trade to the maintenance of artificially high prices by the privileged companies and which maintained that the Dutch were succeeding because of more liberal trading policies [38]. It should be noted, however, that this group did not demand abolition of the companies but rather greater freedom of entry into the charmed circle—as Dr Penelope Corfield has said, they lacked that later faith in the powers of self-regulation of the market itself which stimulated *laissez-faire* policies, continuing to believe in the regulation of trade through the device of companies. Although Charles I reversed the policies of Parliament in the 1630s, even in the 1640s the 'free traders' were prevented from outright opposition because Parliament was receiving aid from the Merchant Adventurers Company. As a result Parliament went so far as to confirm the Company's privileges in 1643.

It is easy to see that for most Englishmen involved in overseas trade the economic crisis involving the cloth trade in the 'old draperies' completely dominated the situation. Yet, as is now clear to historians, the simultaneous rise in the 'new draperies', sold in the warmer lands of the Mediterranean, and the discovery of new markets in the West Indian and American colonies, particularly towards the end of the century, diverted English trade and provided a solution for the crisis in northern European trade.

The first development can be briefly summarised. According to some historians changes in sheep-rearing in sixteenth-century England—the raising of sheep on better grassland—meant that there were no longer adequate supplies of the short fine wool which went to make the 'old draperies' but instead quantities of long coarse wool ideal for the making of lighter woollen cloths and mixtures such as worsteds. In any event the worsted industry became established around 1560—fostered by Protestant refugees from the Netherlands and by a certain amount of demand for worsteds on the home market. Until the end of Anglo-Spanish hostilities, however, the expansion of the industry was contained and its existence was dependent upon a home market. During the early seventeenth century the Italian and Spanish industries were in difficulties and the English managed to capture their market for worsteds, aided by the fact that the Dutch were heavily engaged in war during the 1630s. Almost uninterrupted expansion of the English 'new draperies' for nigh on a century was the consequence although the 'old draperies' dominated the trade until after the Civil War. Merchants, however, were justifiably worried by the fact that these new cloths were much cheaper than the 'old draperies'—far more bulk had to be exported to achieve the same value of export; moreover, at times wool had to be imported from Spain to support the industry. Certainly the English cloth trade was threatened during the seventeenth and eighteenth centuries by the growing demand for lightweight, luxury fabrics such as silk, linen and oriental cottons.

As trade with the New World was of little importance before the Civil War, it provided no immediate answer to England's economic crisis in the 1620s, but later the importance of the trade rose impressively. It was mainly based upon the import and re-export of the colonial commodities of sugar and tobacco. Imports of tobacco rose steeply from 50,000 pounds in 1615 to some 38 million pounds in 1700 and by this later date nearly two-thirds of the tobacco was intended for re-export. England's sugar re-exports dominated northern Europe and demand for sugar increased as coffee drinking became popular, and fresh and dried fruits common. English trade in Asia—not colonially based—was also important. Even before the Civil War there had been modest imports of oriental cottons which were very popular but the post-Civil War period witnessed the real boom in oriental textiles. In 1700 they accounted for some two-thirds of the East India Company's imports. Europeans, alarmed by the threat to the 'new draperies' clamped down restrictions on import of oriental textiles at the turn of the century. The relative lateness of the development in Asian and American trade may be illustrated by the fact that in 1621 combined imports from Asia and the Americas accounted for only 7 per cent of the total, whereas in 1700 they accounted for some 34 per cent of the imports of Great Britain. English domination of the re-export of sugar, tobacco and cottons to Europe was made possible by several factors—the Dutch were prevented by the effectively enforced Navigation Laws from trading on a large scale with England's colonies; France was pre-occupied with internal troubles; the Dutch were less interested in India than in Indonesia and her spices, and did not hinder English trade with India; English/American shipping was sufficiently developed to undertake long-distance, high-bulk trading.

No short chapter can treat the problems of English foreign trade over such a period in detail but this essay has tried to demonstrate some of the reasons why contemporaries felt overseas trade to be important; to show how Englishmen involved in trade were beginning to believe that the possession of a favourable balance of trade was crucial to the nation's wealth—causing a concentration upon export and re-export, an aversion to excessive imports, controversies about the role of government in regulating commerce and of the monopolistic companies in the organisation of commerce itself, and complications in foreign policy and domestic politics; and, finally, to indicate that, whereas the trade with northern Europe in the 'old draperies' was indeed predominant and pre-eminent prior to the Civil War, so that a crisis in this trade was serious indeed, nevertheless England found significant new markets for her own cloth exports during the second half of the century and took over Amsterdam's position as entrepôt for the re-export trade—based in this case largely upon colonial products.

# Extracts

## 1. The Number of Households in the Parishes of Coventry and Lichfield diocese, 1563
(page 11)

### The Deanerie of Derbie

The parochiall churches havinge annexed too them chappells of ease with cure with the names of the same chappells and number of howsholds belonginge to everye of the sayed churches and chappells.

| | |
|---|---|
| The churche of All Saints in Derbie howsholds | – clxxxxiiii |
| The chappell of Querndon howsholds | – xiiii |
| The churche of St. Peters in Derbie howsholds | – cvii |
| The ii chappells of Marston and Bollton howsholds | – xxxvii |
| The churche of St. Michells in Derbie howsholds | – xxx |
| The chappell of Alvaston howsholds | – xx |
| The churche of St. Alkmunds in Derbie howsholds | – |
| The chappell of Lyttell Eyton howsholds | – lxxiiii |
| The churche of Mackworthe howsholds | – liii |
| The chappell of Allestree howsholds | – xxxiiii |
| The churche of Horsley howsholds | – xxxiiii |
| The chappell of Denbye howsholds | – xliiii |
| The churche of Spondon howsholds | – cxvi |
| The chappell of Chaddesden howsholds | – lii |
| The churche of Elvaston howsholds | – lx |
| The chappell of Okenbrooke howsholds | – xxxv |

(B. M. Harleian MS. 594)

# A Summary of the Number of Households in Coventry and Lichfield Diocese, illustrating the distribution of population

## ARCHDEACONRY OF DERBY

| | |
|---|---|
| In the deanrye of Derby howseholdes | – ii$^{m}$ vi$^{c}$ xxxix |
| In the deanrye of Castellarye howseholdes | – vii$^{c}$ xiii |
| In the deanrye of Repingdon howseholdes | – vii$^{c}$ xiii |
| In the deanrye of Heyghe Peake howseholdes | – i$^{m}$ xix |
| In the deanrye of Asheburne howseholdes | – i$^{m}$ vii$^{c}$ lxxxxvii |
| In the deanerye of Scaresdale howseholdes | – ii$^{m}$ v$^{c}$ lxiiii |
| [sum of the archdeaconry of Derby] | – ix$^{m}$ iiii$^{c}$ xliiii |

## ARCHDEACONRY OF SALOP

| | |
|---|---|
| In the deanrye of Salop howseholdes | – iii$^{m}$ iii$^{c}$ xlii |
| In the deanerye of Newporte howseholdes | – i$^{m}$ viii$^{c}$ lviii |
| [sum of the archdeaconry of Salop] | – iiii$^{m}$ viii$^{c}$ lviii |

## ARCHDEACONRY OF STAFFORD

| | |
|---|---|
| In the deanerye of Stone and Newecastell howseholdes | – ii$^{m}$ lvii |
| In the deancrye of Lapleye howseholdes | – i$^{m}$ iii$^{c}$ lxxvii |
| In the deanrye of Tamworthe and Tutbury howseholdes | – i$^{m}$ vii$^{c}$ lviii |
| In the deanerye of Alveton and Leeke howseholdes | – i$^{m}$ vi$^{c}$ xli |
| [sum of the archdeaconry of Stafford] | – vi$^{m}$ viii$^{c}$ xxxiii |

## ARCHDEACONRY OF COVENTRY

| | |
|---|---|
| In the deanerye of Marton howseholdes | – i$^{m}$ xlix |
| In the deanrye of Coventry howseholdes | – i$^{m}$ iii$^{c}$ lii |
| In the deanrye of Arden howseholdes | – ii$^{m}$ v$^{c}$ lii |
| In the deanrye of Stonelye howseholdes | – viii$^{c}$ v |
| [sum of the archdeaconry of Coventry] | – v$^{m}$ vii$^{c}$ xliiii |
| In exempte jurisdictions howseholds | – iiii$^{m}$ iiii$^{c}$ vii |
| [sum total of all] | – xxxi$^{m}$ ii$^{c}$ lxxxvii |

(B. M. HARLEIAN MS. 594)

## 2. Clerical Consolidation of the Glebe Land by Enclosure, 1635

(page 18)

If any one shall in after ages claime any buts or lands, exprest in this terrier . . . let him knowe that the rectorie enioyeth those lands by an exchange made long agoe in the time of the former incumbent & those parties had full satisfaction out of the auncient glebe for them & therefore cannot be taken away without manifest token of sacriledge . . . and we doe not doubt but the curse of god will pursue that man to the utter extirpation of him & his posterity for ever . . .

L.J.R.O. B/V/6/B.19, terrier for Bolas, Salop, 1635

## 3. In Praise of Alternate Husbandry, 1652
(page 17)

There is a parcel of land in Warwickshire, near Stratford upon Avon, that is oaded* every fourteen years, and corned divers years after that. And so there may be many more parcels also besides this I speak of, and so I know there is, and after that fourteen years' rest and grazing, oaded again, and corned also. So there are some in Northamptonshire, Buckinghamshire, and many other parts will do the like. And so runs round, grazing fits for ploughing and corning, and corning fits for grazing; a most gallant opportunity; doubles the grazing rent while under corning and more under oading. And grazeth again immediately at a very considerable rent, and might do the first year at old rent, and so forward, would they plough but three or four years according to my direction, but they plough five, six, or seven. Such a method would please me gallantly, advance the Commonwealth exceedingly, and prejudice whom, I fain would know? Abundance of poor set on work; abundance of corn raised; abundance of straw which spent and fed upon the land shall make that up again whatever the plough fetched out. Doubles rent and more, four or five years in one and twenty. And so every age fetcheth in the purchase.

WALTER BLITH, *The English Improver Improved*, 1652

* wooded.

## 4. Sale of Wool in Yorkshire, 1641
(page 29)

Wee usually sell our wooll att hoame unlesse it bee by chance that wee carry some to Beverley on Midsummer day: those that buy it carry it into the west, towards Leeds, Hallifax and Wakefield; they bring with them packe horses, and carry it away in greate packes; these wool-men come and goe continually from clippinge time till Michaelmasse. Those that have pasture wooll, sell usually for 10s and 11s a stone; and often-times, when woll is very deare, for 12s a stone.
. . . . usually sixe of our ordinary fleeces make a just stone; if the fleeces be very good, five of them will bee a stone, and if they be bad, seaven.

*Farming Book of Henry Best of Emswell*, Surtees Society, xxxiii, 24, 26

## 5. River Avon and Navigation
(page 32)

**17 January 1635/6**

'Att this chamber yt is likewise agreed thatt Mr Mayor, Mr Aldermen, Mr Fareley, Mr Morley, Mr Dauncey and Mr Nash shall meete to-morrowe & consider of the reasons to bee certified unto the Lordes of the Councell wherefore the River of Avon should not bee made navigable. . .'

**7 January 1640/1**

'Att this chamber yt is agreed that Humfry Vernon gent Henry Ford gent Thomas Wildie gent Hugh Greene gent George Heming Nicholas Wildie Thomas Pumfry Richard Barber John Cocksey & Juhn Higgins shall consider of the agreavances & prejudice that this cittie doeth suffer by Mr Sandys his navigation uppon the River Avon and of his ingrossing of corne butter leather fullers earth & many other thinges And that they prepare & certificate thereof to bee certified under the common seale of this cittie unto the house of Parliament.'

*Worcester Chamber Order Book*, transcripts,
Birmingham Reference Library

## 6. New Act against any Person trading in the City of Worcester not a Freeman, 20 March 1617–18

(page 34)

At this chamber it is likewise ordered & agreed by the common councell of this cytty that noe person or persons whatsoever not beinge a freeman of the cytty of Worcester at any tyme after the feast of the Annunciacon next ensuinge shall by himselfe or any other person keepe any shopp or other place for the shewinge or putting to sale of any wares or merchandise by way of engrosse retayle or otherwise neyther shall any person use or exercise any art, trade, occupacon, mystery or handycrafte, whatsoever in this the sayde cyttie or libertyes of the same not beinge a freeman of the sayde citty: upon paine of the forfeiture of the some of 30s for every moneth wherein any person shall soe offende . . . providede that this acte shall not extend to any person for the buyeinge & sellinge of any kind of victuall within the sayed cytty: but that every person may sell the same as heretofore they have usually done.

*Worcester Chamber Order Book*, transcripts

## 7. A Husband and Wife in Kent forced to Live Apart by Poverty, 1636
(page 42)

. . . one Katherine Knight liveth from her husband . . . [when brought before the consistory court she] allegavit that she is with all her heart willing to cohabit with her husband, but for want of meanes to keep house withall together, they are constreined to separate, and live a sunder, each making shift for their owne living, yet they come often together, & he was lately with her once or twice, and should be welcome to her for all if they had wherewithall to maintaine them & keep house. And that her husband is well contented to live thus from her . . .

L.P.L. *Visitation Act Book, 1634–7* (VC III/1/23 f. 233)

## 8. The Norwich Census of the Poor, 1570
(page 42)

Richard Rich of 35 yeris, a husbondman that worke with Mr Cantrell, & kepe not with his wyfe but at tymes & helpeth hyr lyttle, and Margaret his wyf, of 40 yeris, she spynn white warpe, and Jone, ther daughter of 12 yeris, that spyn also the same, & Symond, ther son of 8 yeris, that go to skole, & Alice & Fader, the eldest of 4 & the other 8 yeris. They have dwelt here 2 yeris & syns wyttsontyde, & have dwelt most at Banham wher they were maried, & syns at Swanton next North Walsham & Amringhall. The house of Mr Robert Suklyng. No almes & veri poore. Hable to work. To go away.

Peter Browne, porter, a cobler of 50 yeris, hath lyttle worke, and Agnes his wyfe, of 60 yeris, that worketh nott but hav ben syk syns Christmas, but in helth she spyn white warpe; 3 daughters of 18, 16, of 14 yeris which all spyn when they can get yt, but nowe they ar withoute worke. They have dwelt here above 20 yeris, & they have on daughter, Elizabeth, is idle & sent from cervis with William Naught of Thorp, wher she dwelt 3 quarters of a yer.
hable
The house of the gates. 4d a weke & veri pore. Hable to work. Non spare.

N.N.R.O. *Poor Relief Book, 1571–2*

## 9. The Statute of Artificers, 1563
(page 47)

XVIII. And for the better advuncement of Husbondry and tillage, and to thintente that such as are fyt to be made apprentices to husbondry may be bounden thereunto . . . That every person being an housholder and havinge and usinge halfe a ploughe land at the least in tillage, may have and receyve as an apprentice any person above thage of tenne yeres and under thage of xviii yeres to serve in husbandry untill his age of xxi yeres at the least, or until thage of xxiiii yeres as the parties can agree. . . .

XIX. That every person being an housholder and xxiiiii yeres olde at the least, dwelling . . . in any cytie or towne corporate, and usinge and exercising any arte mysterie or manuell occupacion there, shall and may after the feast of St John Baptist next comynge . . . reteyn the sonne of any freman not occupying husbandry nor beinge a laborer and inhabyting in the same or in any other citie or towne . . . incorporate, to serve and be bounde as an apprentice after the custome and order of the citie of London for seven yeres at the least, so as the tearme and yeares of such apprentice do not expire or determyn afore suche apprentice shalbe of thage of xxiiii yeres at the leaste.

XX. Provided . . . that it shall not be lawful to any person dwellinge in any citie or towne corporate usinge exercysinge any of the mystereis or craftes of a merchante trapheiquinge by trapheke or trade into any partes beyonde the seae, mercer, draper, goldesmith, ironmonger, inbroderer or clothear that dothe or shall put clothe to makynge and saile, to take any apprentices or servaunte to be enstructed or taughte in any of the artes . . . which they . . . exercise, except such servaunt or apprentice be his son, orels that the father or mother of suche apprentice or servaunte shall have . . . landes, tenementes [etc] of the clere yerely value of xls of one estate of inheritance or freeholde at the leaste.

## 10. The Poor Child Register of Southampton, 1609–1637

(page 48)

The names of poore children bound apprentices by the Maior Aldermen and Assistantes of the towne of Southampton for the tyme beinge as followeth, vizt.:

Tempore Philippi Toldervey maioris anno 1609 xxiiii° Novembris 1609

Margerie Lee daughter of John Lee joyner bounde apprentice to John Dewen joyner and Joane his wife for tenn yeres next ensewinge.

x August 1610

Fry Michael s of Robert F to William Martin sergeweaver till age 24. Mr recd 10s.

xii October 1610

Smith Hugh s of Andrew S blacksmith to Nicholas Wools blacksmith for 12 yrs from Mich last. App to have at end 8s and double apparel. Mr recd 8s.

xii April 1611

Helliar Henry s of John H glover to Jo Dale glover for 10 yrs from Mids next. App to have double apparel at end.

xx March 1611/2

Lansdale s of Eustace L to Anthony Searle shoemaker for 8 yrs from L D next. 'In consideracion whereof and of a fine of 20s the Mr is allowed to be a free man of this towne.'

xxiv January 1633/4

Nayler James s of James N of Southton glover aged about 15 . . . to James Barger clothier for 8 yrs from Pur BVM next to be instructed in woolcombing and weaving. App to have at end 5s and double apparel. Mr to have 20s. If app die within 1 yr, Mr to restore half the money.

i November 1637

Elliott John s of Henry E aged 6 to Stephen Parker tailor for 15 yrs from Pur BVM next. Mr has promised to cause him to be taught to read and write, as well as the trade of tailor. App to have double apparel at end. Mr recd 51s and will restore 50s if he or app dies within 1 yr. Signed by Mr.

A. J. WILLIS and A. L. MERSON, *Southampton Corporation MS.* SC 9/2/13. *A Calendar of Southampton Apprentice Registers,* 1609–1740, Southampton University 1968

*Abbreviations*

| | |
|---|---|
| app | apprentice |
| s | son |
| Mr | Master |
| recd | received |
| L D | Lady Day |
| Pur BVM | Feast of the Purification of the Blessed Virgin Mary. |

## 11. A Concession to de-mobbed Soldiers regarding Apprenticeship, 1654

(page 50)

We have considered the petition of several officers of his Highness's army, the same setting forth that divers persons having been officers and soldiers of the army in their youth and desiring now (being reduced) to betake themselves to honest callings find themselves interrupted therein by privileges granted to corporations for debarring persons from exercising any art, etc., there without seven years' apprenticeship.

And are humbly of opinion that every person who shall make it appear he hath served in the late wars in England, Scotland or Ireland by the space of three years at any time since the year 1642 and before the ...... day of ...... in the year 1653, though not bound apprentice or not serving up his time, be at liberty to set up and exercise any art, mystery, trade, or manual occupation he shall think fit and be capable of in any city, town, or place in this commonwealth, notwithstanding any law, custom, or privilege to the contrary. And if any such person shall be sued or molested for the same by any information, action of debt, or other popular action, and shall prove that he hath been a soldier for the space of three years, and the jury shall find him not guilty and the plaintiff shall in that case pay him double costs. And that an ordinance be brought in to that purpose.

P.R.O., SP 18/74, no. 37

## 12. Knowledge in our mother tongue by reading of the Scriptures, by comming to the Church, by hearing of Diuine Service and word of God preached, is farre better then ignorance in the Latine, Greeke, or Hebrew which is not understood

(page 51)

Many a man is ignorant of the Gospel, because he hath never beene taught it; And this is the darknesse in which naturall men delight. . . . But this ignorance is banished by education, and the excellent means of divine instruction.

I. BOURNE, *The True Way of a Christian*, 1622

## 13. William Day, Provost of Eton, in a Sermon at Paul's Cross, 1566

(page 53)

. . . they be taken from the universities after they have been their a whill and sent unto the lawes of the Realme wheras their is such a nomber as I understand that the howses can not receave them. I would wishe their might be some order taken for the law as it was for the monkes, for when they so increased that the houses could not hold them and every man sought to be a monke their was a certen nomber appoynted to every house above the which he should not passe. And wheras god shold have the fayrest and the best appoynted for him, their is now none but the hault and lame put to the ministrey which can make no better and other shifte.

Bodleian Library, Oxford, MS. Tanner 50

## 14a. Queen Elizabeth to the Lord Keeper, Nicholas Bacon, 1560
(page 53)

We understand that the study of divinity is much decayed in our Universities. . . ., by lack of provisions for the students through late alterations, so that many leave the Universities. The Chancellors therefore are to send you a schedule of the most towardly divinity students that have need of exhibition, and you shall in our name confer on them all prebends in your disposition for one year, or longer if required, till there be some repair of this lamentable lack.

C.S.P.D. *Addenda, Elizabeth, 1547–65*, vol. ix, no. 77

## 14b. Andrew Perne, Vice-Chancellor of Cambridge, to Sir William Cecil, with reference to the Queen's order, 1560
(page 53)

The cheerfulness of the students on the news shows that they do not lack goodwill for the study of theology, but had gone to law or medicine for fear of want. I send you the lists, but I hope that many will now transfer themselves to the deserted study of theology. There was never a larger number of learned youths, but poverty had often made their studies mercenary, and deterred them from theology. This plague is taken away by the Queen's letters, showing that theology is had in more honour than the other arts, and will not lack rewards.

C.S.P.D. *Addenda, Elizabeth, 1547–65*, vol. ix, no. 78

## 15. Will of Gervase Sleigh, Merchant, of the Town of Derby, dated 1624
(page 55)

Item for that my sonne Gervas is nowe student at Christ colledge in Cambridge, and that my desire is to breede him a scholler I doe therefore give and bequeath to him for his better maintenaunce there out of all my lands within the Lordshippe of Ashe and Dalbury, the yearlie rent of twenty pounds to beginne ymediatlie after my decease for and untill he shall accomplish the age of twenty and two yeares, to be returned to Cambridge for him at the end of every halfe yeare tenn pounds trulie and duely untill his age of two and twentie yeares as aforesaid. . . . [Gervase the elder added certain other rents to this bequest and instructed his executors to pay Gervase the younger out of these rents a further £10 p.a. towards his better maintenance at Cambridge] 'or more if they shall perceave and finde good cause therefore for his Commencement or other needful occasions'.

Item my will and minde is that my sonne Hugh Sleigh shalbe trained upp at Repton or some other good schoole in learninge and writinge and castinge accompts with penn and compters And alsoe in the art of Arethmeticke untill he shall accomplishe the age of seaventeene or eighteene yeares, to make him fitt for a London prentice And I doe allott and give twentie marks every yeare out of my whole estate for his maintenaunce duringe that time . . . Item my will and minde is that my Executors and freinds . . . shall putt my said sonne Hugh to be prentice in London to serve eight or nyne yeares either with a marchant or some tradesman, where he maye bee vertuously brought up to learne his duty to God and man, that so if it shall please God he maye prove a necessary member in the Commonwealth and a comfort to his friends. . . .

Item my will is that there shalbe allowed out of the profitts of all my lands and whole estate personall and reall . . . for to maintaine sonne Samuell the heir at Graies Inne where he nowe is, fiftie pounds per annum untill he shall attaine the age of twenty and one yeares. . . .

[All three sons (Samuel, Gervase and Hugh) attended Repton school. Samuel left at the age of 18 and matriculated at Christ's College, Cambridge (1621), where he spent 2 years. He left without taking a degree and entered Gray's Inn, London in October 1623.

Gervase left Repton in 1623 at age 15 and entered Christ's in the same year. In providing him with support until age 22 his father was enabling him to complete the traditional full seven-year course.]

P.C.C. *Will of Gervase Sleigh*, 1624

## 16. Excerpts from the Bagot Family Papers
(page 57)

7 June 1589: Richard Bagot to his son Walter

'. . . Allso Mr Brook of Hasallor is a sutor to me to have some Roome or chamber in the manor for ther ar iiiir of his children that shold go to skoole ther, I will have you to go and view the howse ther, in what sort it is and if ther be any chamber convenyent, to let Mr. Broke have it, and to kepe it in good order, that he mak no wast . . . .

*The Bagot Papers*, Folger Library

## 17. An Episcopal Instruction to Check the Licences of Schoolmasters, and to Review the Same, 1584

(page 58)

[Article 14] Whether you have a schoolmaster in your parish, and whether your schoolmaster teaching publicly or privately be of good and sincere religion and conversation; and whether they be examined and allowed by the ordinary [=bishop] or his officer in that behalf; and whether any living given towards the erection or maintenance of any school be witholden back, or otherwise any ways employed?

[All schoolmasters are ordered to] bring in their licences before to them granted the third day of the first month next after the visitation [to the bishop] to whome if they do not sufficiently allow their ability for learning, their soundness for religion, their honesty for conversation by learning and testimony of such as are well known to the bishop, then to be displaced and inhibited to continue their teaching any longer within this diocese.

W. P. M. Kennedy (ed.), *Elizabethan Episcopal Administration*, Alcuin Club Collections (1924)

(27,165, being Visitation Article 14; & 143, being extract from *Certain Advertisements*, 1584; both relating to the diocese of Coventry and Lichfield)

## 18. Accounts of a Staffordshire Coal-mine
(page 65)

| | |
|---|---|
| Candelles spente this yeare lx dozen xviii poundes | xii$^{li}$ |
| Tymber mens wages this yeare | vii$^{li}$ |
| Payed to the two Otties for sawinge tymber for the coale pyttes . . . at ixd the daye | v$^{li}$ vid |
| Payed for roopes for the pyttes this yeare | xxvs |
| Payed for bowkes and trunckes this yeare | vs |
| Payed for sinkinge xii pyttes this yeare | vi$^{li}$ |
| Sum of the payments and allowances | xxx$^{li}$ xs vid |
| Coales sent to Burton this yeare | xxiii loades |
| Summa totalis clear gotten at the coales pyttes this yeare all thinges discharged | lxxviii$^{li}$ xvis viiid |

[The accounts also include wages for miners not given here.]

S.C.R.O. D(W) 1734/3/3/252

## 19. Leeds Clothiers Resist Incorporation in a Gild, 1629
(page 70)

Sheweth, that whereas it pleased your most excellent Majesty by your letters patents dated the 12 day of July in the second year of your Majesty's most happy reign to incorporate the said town and parish for the better increase of the trade of clothing. And your Highness's said letters patents did give liberty and power to all the said parishioners and inhabitants to distinguish and divide themselves into gilds and fraternities, not giving authority to the aldermen and assistants there to enforce or compel any to be companies unless they willingly submitted thereunto. So it is, may it please your most excellent Majesty, that the present Alderman . . . and a few of the chief burgesses for the increase of their own authority and for their own gain . . . and not for the good of clothing contrary to the goodwill and liking of most and of the best of the parish (there being not the fortieth part of the clothiers that do consent thereunto as the petitioners hope to make it appear) endeavour to enforce the petitioners to be a company and to submit themselves to such rules and constitutions as they shall please to make, to be fined, imprisoned, and called from their labour at their wills.

Your petitioners shew that many of them daily setting on work above forty poor people in their trade, and that compelling them to come hither, dwelling 150 miles hence, tendeth much to their impoverishing and overthrow of their trade.

And therefore your petitioners humbly pray that your Majesty would be graciously pleased to refer the examination as well of the consent and allowance of those whom this business doth concern as the consideration of the inconveniency of the thing that is desired by the said Alderman . . . [etc] as shall seem best to your Majesty and who best understand the nature of clothing.

From petition printed in J. J. CARTWRIGHT,
*Chapters in the History of Yorkshire*, Wakefield, 1872

## 20. A Proposal to Regulate the Rural Cloth Industry, 1625
(page 73)

.... That the justices of peace by name of the county be all incorporated by the name of the Governors for the New Drapery of that county, to them and their successors, justices of the peace of that county.
That these Governors be enabled with power to make laws and ordinances for the advancing of this trade and to choose officers.
To raise stocks.
To inflict punishment upon offenders.
To take account and dispose of all things for the public utility of the county.
That the body of the incorporation to be all the inhabitants of or within the county.
All ordinary clauses for corporations to be added.
A special clause to follow the directions of his Majesty and his lands.
Directions to the governors to be expressed for the present in a schedule to be annexed to the Letters Patents.
These to be varied from time to time as there shall be occasion by the advice of the Lords of the Council signified under the seal of the Council, and to be registered by the clerk of the company in their register or repertory.
The present directions to be: for the length of every piece to be constant 27 yards; for the breadth to be for broad stuff ......; for narrow ......; for the weight ...... For the searches and trials every piece shall pass from the weaver, from the fuller, from the rower or clothworker, from the dyer, from the presser for the several seals. No fees to any officers but out of the forfeitures.

P.R.O. SP 16/1, no. 24
(An earlier version of this proposal was made by Walter Morrell of Herts, in December 1622)

## 21. The Farming Stock of a reasonably prosperous Clerical Mixed Farmer in Leicestershire, December 1672

(page 77)

| | |
|---|---|
| In the cheese chamber Item one frame to lay cheese upon & shelves & tressells in the said roome | 10s. 00d |
| In the back kitchen item one cheesepress one churne one forme one thrawle two window shutts one little table one kinnell & milke briggs one sheefe one pair of weights & one little tressle | 10s. 00d |
| ... In the yard item 9 beasts at $ii^{li}xs$ a peece | 22. 10s. 00d |
| Item two foles | 5. 00s. 00d |
| Item one rack & hanger on the back side the barne | 2s. 00d |
| Item wheat rye & barly in the barne | 15. 00s. 00d |
| Item one fanne to winnow with & a wheel & one ladder & one scuttle and one carte | 4. 00s. 00d |
| Item the pease on the hovell | 4. 10s. 00d |
| Item one ladder two cribbs | 10s. 00d |
| Item the hovell timber | 1. 00s. 00d |
| Item 8 hoggs | 3. 10s. 00d |
| Item 3 calves | 1. 00s. 00d |
| Item one ladder one rack | 02s. 00d |
| Item hey in the barn & lumber over the cowhowse | 12. 00s. 00d |
| Item 5 yearling heifers at | 3. 00s. 00d |
| Item two cribbs in wollatts close | 03s. 00d |
| Item oates & pease in St Johns howse | 1. 13s. 04d |
| Item one well curbe buckett & chain | 05s. 00d |
| Two hogg troughs & a wheelbarrow | 03s. 00d |
| In the stable item 5 horses & mares | 15. 00s. 00d |
| Item 4 paire of geares one cartrope | 1. 08s. 00d |
| Item two saddles & bridles one shovell one spade one pack saddle & a paire of panniers & one barr of iron. | 10s. 00d |
| In the clovergrass close item two stacks of hey | 12. 00s. 00d |
| Item 39 sheep of severall sorts | 5. 00s. 00d |
| Item eight strike of pease | 16s. 00d |
| Item 11 strike of barly | 16s. 00d |
| Item 3 strike of wheat | 09s. 00d |

| | |
|---|---|
| Item 6 strike of rye | 12s. 00d |
| Item XI acres of wheat growing upon the gleab land in the feild | 16. 10s. 00d |
| Item a lease of certain lands in Ashover in the county of Derby formerly purchased of Sir Samuel Tryon wherein the executrix hath her life to the value of about 12li per annum. | 40. 00s. 00d |
| Item in good debts owinge | 40. 00s. 00d |

[The total estate, including household effects, books and other sundry items such as the furnishings of brewery and buttery, was appraised at £309 04s. 10d, and this despite the fact that the Rector concerned had been impoverished by plundering troops during the Civil War to the amount of £500. It should be noted that the inventory was taken in winter when stock (both arable and livestock) was presumably at its lowest.]

L.C.R.O. *The Inventory of Immanuel Bourne,*
Rector of Aylestone, Leicestershire, 1672

## 22. A Clerical Farmer's Record of Climate and Harvest, 1632
(page 78)

Corne rose much in price before in the harvest 1632. A very good faier hey harvest at first, after much raine & then a very faier corne harvest beginning in September & continued faier till 15 of September then much raine hindered harvest which was very backward in most places, then from 22 to Mychaelmas very fine faier whether for ending of whete corne & we began the pulse till 22 some small pulse & then about Michaelmas we began to cut big pulses, carried none to any purpose till after Michaelmas . . . [but the pulse harvest was partially ruined by rain in mid October].
This was an extraordinary backward harvest of all manner of graine as ever was, harvest of fruit small & backward & no great stoare, no grapes ripe now at all, we stowed no winter corne till October 29 & then it was a fine steding by the 9 of November.
Great stoare of pulse this yeare but much spoiled before it was inned.
Few or no small nuts. I stow out a waspe 1632.

Corne rose much in April 1633 a very unkindly barly seeding & very unseasonable weather April 18 being [?] Thursday the grownd was covered with snowe. A passing rainy time till . . . May & then it was very dry & fayer with no raine at all from April 23 to May 19, then some raine after. In June much raine & our meades much drowned. Corne rose, especially barly & pulses in June etc.

A very backward harvest, we began to mowe our meadowes August 19 1633. No corne harvest till September.
A little Lammas wheate croped August 27.
Harvest not ended with us till St Lukes daie, in other places not so soone, barly very bad every where, never known to be worse nore more [?] & unkindly, wheat good in show but bad in yeld & not kindly ripe, nor any fruit, no grapes ripened, no filbards, fewe old nuts . . . barly was sold in October & November, the best 30s a quarter. Sheep rotte in most places, almost all sheep died about us & throughout England. 1633.

A very kindly barly seedling from March 10th to [?] no raine but passing dry 1634.

No raine at all byt passing dry & for the most part hard frost & very cold from March 10 to Aprill the tenth & then it rained & the wind for most part was east 1634.
The last of December 1633 being new yeares eve was a fearefull earthquake in & about Hereford.
This year 1634 corne fell much, in May barly sold for 22s at Abingdon, some under; wheat under 5s, maslin 3s. 4d.
A very kindly May, dry most part from 19 to third very dry & fyer & very dry & fyer & exceeding hot summer [sic].

Bodleian Library, Oxford, MS. Top. Oxon. c.378.
*Diary of Thomas Wyatt*, Rector of Ducklington (Oxon) 1622–49
(with modernised punctuation)

## 23. A Merchant of Bristol Loans Money, 1660
(page 87)

8 December 1660.
William Crabb of the said city, merchant, maketh oath that before the ship Hare of Bristol, burden fifty tons or thereabouts, set sail last from the port of Bristol in her last voyage, he the deponent did let out at interest unto several persons certain sums of money payable again unto him at the return of the said ship to the port of Bristol that voyage with interest therefore, and the deponents had bonds of them for the same to the value of near forty pounds, and by reason of a loss of the said ship in Ireland the same principal money and interest remain all unsatisfied to this deponent....

PATRICK MCGRATH, *Merchants and Merchandise in Seventeenth Century Bristol,* Bristol Record Society, XIX, 1955, p. 189

## 24. The Activities of a Financial and Business Agent in London in the 1660s
(pages 88 and 90)

June 1663
I do acknowledge to have in my hands the sume of one thousand pounds of Mr. Alexander Courthope's money to be put out for him upon good security if it may be or otherwise to pay it as he shall direct, witness my hand this day and year abovesaid. } £1,000

[signed] Hump. Tuckey

September 1663
I have secured you money very well by taking plate and jewells of a goldsmith for it to the value of 11 hundred pound which I conceive far better than a note of a servant's hand. You are to have £4. 10s. per cent per annum for 3 months from the 20th August last and on 30 dayes warning to pay in the money. I have the plate in custody.

September 1666 [Consequences of the Great Fire and note of use of Sir Robert Viner as banker.]
I must begg your pardon if I write noncence for I am in a sadd condition, my home burnt. . . . as were all my other houses in London to the value of £150 per annum; but as to your accompts all is safe only I have £500 in Sir Robert Viner's hands, how they disposed of their cash I know not but will make enquiry.

K.C.R.O. *Courthope Letters*

## 25. Property Sales in the 17th Century
(page 89)

[Land belonging to Sir Edward Hales, with rents per annum of £1,125, timber of per annum value £1,000, 2 manorial courts and 1 advowson, advertised for sale and noted as having the following advantages:]

The premises ly adjacent to each other and are the best tenanted of any estate in the county of Kent lying within foure miles of Maidstone, a very greate and good markett town. All the houses in excellent repaire and soe to be kept by the tennants. And many of them capable of being made with lyttle charge commodious seats for any gentleman, being very faire houses having good accommodations of wood and water and good meadow grounds.

[Sir John Mayney wrote to Mr Morris and Mr Clayton, scriveners, giving details of his land:]

to be mortgaged for £3000 for 4 to 5 years. It is now mortgaged for £4000 of which there is £1,000 paid.

[Clayton and Morris appear to have been approached to advance money on security of property for industrial investment. In connection with a salt-works in 1669 it was:]

proposed to borrow £1,000 upon this worke and for the security to have all the worke in possession till such time as the interest & principall be paid and for further security there shall nothing of this money be expended but for the advancement of the worke so that the lender has the effects of his thousand pounds in his hands for further security.

K.C.R.O. Clayton MSS, *Business files of Robert Clayton and John Morris*, c. 1650–1700

## 26. The Cholmleys of Whitby make arrangements to settle their debts
(page 90)

After much land sold, and debts still increasing, and having a numerous issue, he confined himself to a proportion; and turning the land into the hand of his eldest son (then married) for the payment of debt, and increase of his children's portions; and about the 58th year of his age retired with his wife and family into the city of York, where he continued to his death. [Then the eldest son, Sir Richard Chomley, himself indebted,] . . . made over to [Sir Hugh] the whole estate for ten years, for payment of the said debts, reserving only £400 per annum for himself for that time, and then lived retired at Whitby.

*Cholmley Memoirs*, 15,42

## 27. Provision for Repayment of a Loan, 1621
(pages 95 and 96)

Whereas Sir Baptist Hicks, knight and barronett, Sir William Cockaine and Sir Peter Vanlorre, knightes, upon instance made by their Lordshipps unto them in his Majestie's name, consented to provide and take upp upon their credittes the summe of thirtie thousand poundes which his Majestie was pleased to consigne over to his sonne in law, the Prince Palatine, towardes the reliefe of his army and the recoverie of his ancient inheritance in the Palatinate; and the said monies being accordingly provided and their Lordshipps with the rest of the Councell being to enter into bond to the said knightes for their security, his Majestie's pleasure is that for the indemnity of their Lordships and each of them that are thus to be ingaged for his Majestie's service, the Lord High Treasurer of England doe cause the foresaid summe of 30000 li with the interest for the same to be satisfied and repaid to the foresaid knightes as it shall grow due out of the first monies that shall come into his Majestie's receipt either by subsidie or otherwise and that an Act of Councell be made thereunto and entred into the register of Councell causes for the due performance of the same accordingly.

*Acts of the Privy Council*, 1621–3

## 28. The Relief of La Rochelle
(page 96)

At Whytehall the 1 of June, 1628
Present: The King's Majestie

Lord Treasurer, Lord President, Lord Admirall, Lord Steward, Lord Chamberlaine, Earl of Suffolk, Earl of Dorsett, Earl of Salisbury, Earl of Totnes, Lord Viscount Conwey, Lord Weston, Lord Bishop of Winton, Master of the Wards, Mr. Chancellor of the Duchie.

It was this day thought fitt and ordered that the 3000 li., parte of the 18000 li., remaynder of the loane of monyes from the Cittie, formerly assigned for the payment of the revenue of cntertainement to the trayne of artillery in the late expedicion for Retz, should be now assigned to Sir Sackville Crowe, Treasurer of the Navy, the moyetie whereof is to be by him issued by the way of imprest to the masters and owners of the shipps taken up and to be imployed in his Majesty's fleete for the relieving of Rochell; whereof the Lord Treasurer and the Lord Weston, Chancellor of the Exchequer, are hereby prayed and required to take knowledge, and to give speedie and effectuall order accordingly.

*Acts of the Privy Council*, 1627–8

## 29. The Third Commission to Sell Crown Lands, 1543
(page 106)

. . . . Whereas divers manors, lands, [etc] by sundry and divers ways and means, as by act of parliament, attainder, surrenders and otherwise, are come to us and be in our hands and possession, part thereof, by the advice of our Council, we think meet and convenient, towards the supportation and relief of our great charges being presently at hand to be employed for the defence, maintenance, and safeguard of this our realm and the common wealth of our loving subjects inhabiting the same, to put to sale, divide, distribute, and impart amongst the said our loving subjects, to such as intend to purchase and buy the same of us, and for certain other causes and considerations us specially moving. For accomplishment whereof know ye that we, trusting in your service, fidelities, and approved wisdoms, have appointed and assigned you eight, seven, six, five, or four of you, whereof you the said Sir Richard Rich Chancellor of the Court of Augmentations or you the said Sir Richard Southwell General Surveyor of lands or you the said Sir Edward North Treasurer of the Court of Augmentations to be one, and by these our present letters patent do give unto you . . . full power and authority to bargain and sell and fully to conclude and agree for us in our name to our said subjects such of our said manors, [etc] being as well within the survey of our said court of augmentations . . . as of our said court of General Surveyors of our lands, amounting in the whole to the whole and clear yearly value of ten thousand pounds or under as shall seem to you . . . most meet and convenient by your discretions. The same bargains and sales not to be made of any one manor, farm or other hereditaments being certified to you by the auditor thereof to exceed the clear yearly value forty pounds . . . The same bargains and sales of the premises not before excepted . . . [and with the exception, also, of lands and property in London or other cities, boroughs and towns, and of property granted for life or lives without rent] to be made after the rate of twenty years' purchase at the least, or more by your discretions, according to the particular values and certificates thereof to be made by the said auditor of the same, which said values and certificates made by them or any of them as is aforesaid shall be a sufficient warrant and discharge to you . . . at all times for the value thereof. . . .

P.R.O., *Chancery, Patent Roll* (C 66) 739, m.19

# 30. Particulars for Grants of Monastic Land
(page 106)

Part of the possession of the late priory of Brewood in the county of Staffordshire:
Brewood . . . it is valued in a rent of assize or free rent from John Moseley for his lands there, per annum, 1d; . . . from Thomas Johnson, 7d; the farm of a pasture there called Dawploke, let to Roger Fowke by indenture, so it is said, at a rent per annum of 1d [Total] 9d Horsebrook and Stretton . . . it is valued in a rent of assize or free rent from Richard Whitmore . . . 3d; for a parcel of land or a croft there, let to Richard Bromehall at the will of the lord, per annum 8d; . . . a messuage with land, meadow, pasture . . . let to John Tomkyns, so it is said, at a rent of 16s Total 16s 11d

Sum Total 17s 8d

Memorandum, the King's highness hath no more land nor tenements in Brewood and Horsebrook belonging to the late monastery other than above mentioned, to the Auditor's knowledge
Item, the premises lieth not nigh any of the King's majesty's houses, forests, chases and parks which be kept for the access of his highness, to the Auditor's knowledge
Item, there be no spiritual promotions belonging to the premises
Item, there have been no other particulars delivered of the premises heretofore
Memorandum, for the woods and underwoods growing on the premises

Examined by Robert Burgoyne [Auditor]

[?] day of March . . . [1545] for John Leveson of Wolverhampton, Merchant:
The rents and farms in Brewood in the county of Stafford, 9d, and in Horsebrook and Stretton in the same county, 16s 11d, in all by the year, parcel of the possession of the late priory of Brewood in the said county, 17s 8d; which rated at 20 years' purchase doth amount to the sum of £17. 13s. 4d, to be paid all in hand
Woods: nil The tenure in socage
Memorandum, the King's majesty must discharge the premises of all incumbrances except leases, and except such charges as the tenants and farmers are bound to discharge
[signed] William St John Robert Southwell Edward North

[woods] . . . will hardly suffice for timber to repair the houses standing upon the same . . . nil

Examined by me David Clayton [Surveyor of the woods]

P.R.O. E318,711]

[being particulars for a grant of former monastic lands in Staffordshire and Shropshire to John Leveson of Wolverhampton, merchant (wool trader)]

# 31. Temporalities of the Diocese of Lichfield, 1623
(pages 115 and 116)

Eccleshall Mannor in County Stafford where the Castle is the bishops usuall place of residence. The tenures there are of diverse sorts; as coppiholds, most of inheritance (but finable . . . .) Leases, for yeares as the Elmdons, lives; Composicion etc; coppyholds by custom.

Lichfield Mannor in the county aforesaid. This mannor with the mills was last of all demised by Bishop Overton to Queen Elizabeth (by the procurement of Robert Earl of Essex) & so passed over to the Citie of Lichfield (viz the Bayliffs & Burgesses) in fee farme for ever. It was of the yearly rent of 57$^{li}$ 3s 1d now only L$^{li}$ so there is vii$^{li}$ iiis id in defectu The old Earl of Essex had, and Robert the now Earl holds them during life.

Brewde mannor & park in the county aforesaid, leased by Bishop Neale for 3 lives unto Walter Gifford Esquire, besides the rent there is only reserved 2 fee bucks & 2 fee does of the season.

Prees mannor in county Salopp It was lett 4 Edward 6 February 16 to commence at Michaelmas before 1550 for 80 years which lease is still on foote, & Sir George Mainwaring farmer. But Bishop Neale made a concurrant lease thereof Anno 1611 20 January for 21 years. The former lease ends 1629 at Michaelmas.

Sawley mannor in county Derby Lett in fee farme for ever; the now farmer is Philip Lord Stanhope Earl of Chesterfield. It is now in defect of the old Rent 33$^{li}$ 10s 10d.

Wibunbury Mannor in County Cheshire Lett by Thomas the Bishop in 1621 to Sir Thomas Smith knight for 3 lives, with an increase of 4$^{li}$ 14s 7d yearly, having bought Bishop Neales concurrant lease before.

L.J.R.O. *Temporalia Episcopalis*, CC 124100

# 32. Observations touching Concurrant Leases, Copyholds and Leases, 1623
(page 115 and 116)

1. If the ancient rent be not reserved upon any such lease, yearly payable, then is the lease void by statute 1 Elizabeth notwithstanding another rent upon the first lease.

2. If there be a clause of re-entry upon any such (or other lease) then in the demand must be observed theese 3 circumstances. vizt. 1° Tempus, the last hower of the day in the lease expressed in which account are reckoned but only 28 daies to a moneth.
2° Locus. Upon the land, and at the howse, (if there be anie on it) & at the doores most used in that howse.
3° Modus, in thees or the like woords
I, N, doo here demand now such a rent due upon such a lease in the presence of such wittnesses, and this may be done personally or by lettre of atturney.

N.B. No concurrant lease is good withoute the confirmation of the Deane and Chapter and unles it commence in the habendum from the making thereof.
Item leases made before 1 Elizabeth confirmed by dean & chapter were good: not so by President & chapter.

TOUCHING COPYHOLDS

If a tenant surrenders at the hands of other customarie tenants and they testifie not the surrender in court . . . . then doo they forfeit their owne estate of coppihold.

If anie tenant be obstinate & will not offer a reasonable fine, the best way is to admit him tenant, and then the steward in open court may impose any fine under 2 yeares value, prefixing a reasonable day for the payment thereof. On which day if the Lords Bailie or any other by lettre of atturney demand the fine, & he neglect the payment, he shall forfeit his copiehold. Wheerupon the Lord by his steward may grant it to anie other in Court, and upon a license to lett & sett he may demise it to any other, who turning in his horse or other wise making his entrie . . . shall recover the land by an ejectione firma. All which was adiudged by all the iudges of the land for Robert Bishop of Hereford against Thomas

Morris of Lindon: & his copiehold land made lease for 3 lives; and can never be copie hold againe.

LEASES

If the habendum be from the day of the date, it is void by the statute 1 Elizabeth which in no case (except marriage) doth commence till the morrow after.
In all such cases 1) if the liverie and seasin were given upon the day of the date, it was too soone. 2) If upon anie day after, by lettre of atturney from the Bishop it is void, and comes too late; and only good when the Bishop doth execute the liverie in person. But if it be from the making theerof or from the date heerof (and not from the day of the date etc) then it is good by lettre of atturney either upon the day or anie day after.
So is a lease void, if there be another unsurrendered up at the making thereof: which althoughe anie bishop could not avoyd (it being his owne act, & good against him) by making another lease, yet his successor might.

L.J.R.O. *Legal observations touching tenure of the Bishop of Lichfield's temporal properties*, CC 124100

## 33. A Letter from the Privy Council to the Suffolk JPs, 1622

(page 125)

Whereas upon the humble information of Samuel Salmon, of Creating in the county of Suffolke, that having for about 30 yeares used the trade of cloathing and therein imployed about 200 people and being of late become indebted by reason of the decay of cloathing and great losses received by suertishipp, badd debtors and otherwise, he was much pressed by some of his creditors to give present satisfaction, which without some respitt of time he was not able to do, it pleased his Majestie to appoint you with some others commissioners, to mediate with the creditors of the said Salmon for some equitable agreement. And whereas it appeareth by your late letters addressed unto us that upon calling of his creditors before you the said Salmon did offer to pay unto them all their due debtes excepting interest money and costes of sute in three yeares next insuing by even portions and thereof to give good security, of which divers of the creditors having accepted, some few others did refuse the same, though their debtes were for money borrowed upon interest and that sundry of them have received as much for use as the principall first lent; forasmuch as you have also certified that the whole estate of the said Salmon will not extend to give further satisfaction than is offered, that he alwaies lived with good reputacion and done good service in that country, that at this present he doth sett on worke 200 poore people that have no other dependance or means of livelihood; lastly that the poore people of that county being great numbers are likely to suffer much distresse if in the present decay of cloathing the honest cloathier be not countenanced, wee have beene mooved for these considerations, hereby to authorise and require you to call before you such of the creditors of the said Salmon as have not already agreed and to treate effectually with them to accept of his honest and reasonable offers and the rather in respect of these our letters of recommendacions which wee have granted unto him as a person who (in these times) wee hold fitt to be cherished and supported by all lawful meanes, seeing the suddaine casting of soe many poore people as depend upon him may proove of ill consequence and that by late directions of the Board the cloathiers are commaunded not to put away their workemen untill they have first acquainted us therewith. . . .

*Acts of the Privy Council*, 1621–3

## 34. The Decay of Trade
(page 132)

28 February 1620/1.
A threefold assertion that the pretermitted custom is not the cause of the decay of trade:
1. The pretermitted custom is by God's law warranted to be taken and paid.
2. It is warranted to be taken and paid by the laws of the land.
3. It was given to his Majesty as well by the merchants themselves as others in the first year of his Majesty's reign towards his Highness's great charge in keeping the narrow seas for preservation of the realm and for intercourse of merchandise.

The causes of the decay of trade:
1. The untimely project of dyeing and dressing of cloths before transportation.
2. The bad making of cloths in the reign of Ed.4 caused foreign nations to burn our cloths and of latter times the French king to burn them.
3. The sending of our wools out of England, Wales, Scotland, and Ireland into foreign parts.
4. The wars in Christendom.
5. The merchant strangers calling in their money and desisting from trade upon their censure in the Star Chamber for transporting coin.
6. The small fellowship of the Hamburg merchants in comparison they were in former years, whereby they are less able to vent our home commodities.
7. The goodness of our coin whereby it is transported by stealth and made over by exchange.
8. The plague of pestilence in the Eastland country which continues to the great loss of all merchants trading thither especially the merchants of the northern parts . . .

Special observations:
. . . For there is made 360,000 cloths in a year whereof 140,000 are yearly transported, and the residue being 220,000 cloths are worn in the realm, whereby his Majesty loseth of the ancient due which divers of his noble progenitors had when wool was transported in kind 110,000 li a year,

which the commons gain for all that charge they were at when the cloths worn in the realm were made beyond the seas and afterwards imported...

Bodleian Library, Oxford, MS. North a2, ff. 241–2

## 35. A Letter from the Privy Council to the Lord Treasurer, 11 September 1621
(page 133)

Wee have thought good for speciall reasons to pray your lordshipp hereby to direct your letters to the officers of the customes, requireing them to certifie the Board what commodities are brought into this realme out of the United Provinces of the Low Countries in the greatest proportion, either native of those partes or of other kindes, and in their report soe to distinguish them, that the one may be knowne and discerned from the other....

*Acts of the Privy Council*, 1621–3

## 36. Trade to Amsterdam, 1638

(page 133)

The trade of this city is much enlarged since the passage of Antwerp was stopped, and the trade of the inhabitants to the East and West Indies, occasioned by their industry, their love to navigation, and not the least by a great plenty of monies which they deliver out at easy rates at interest as wanting land or other means to put out the same to better benefit, nothing being left them but commerce and navigation to employ the same, and of late days England and other neighbouring countries are found to have their estate going at interest according to the custom of the place, which is 8 per cent, whereas in their own countries 4 and 5 per cent is as much as the same will yield them. . . .

LEWES ROBERTS, *The Merchants Mapp of Commerce*, 1638, II, pp. 110

## 37. Clothiers of Ipswich forbidden by the Privy Council to ship goods overseas contrary to the Charters of the Merchant Companies, 1621

(page 135)

Memorandum. This daie according to their Lordships' order, Thomas Hayles, Isaac Day and George Raymond, clothiers of Ipswich, entred into bondes unto his Majestie's use to make their appearance from time to time before their Lordships within two daies after warning given unto them and further that from henceforth they would forbeare to shipp any goodes to be transported beyond the seas, contrarie to the charters of the merchantes and in prejudice of their trade.

*Acts of the Privy Council*, 1621–3

# 38. Reasons for the Decay of the Cloth Trade, 1622
(page 136)

The causes of the decay of the trade of clothing, etc., with remedies:

1. Of the first, the price of wools in the hands of the wool grower is no cause, for that wools are fallen the third or fourth part in price.

2. Neither is the clothier any cause for that they sell their cloth unto the merchant under the price of former times and yet they cannot sell the whole manufacture for the merchant will not take the cloth at the same low prices which the clothier is able to afford, although he sell his cloth now 30li in the hundred cheaper than in former times.

3. Therefore the cause resteth in the buying and ventage of the cloth into and out of the merchants' hands by the privilege granted unto certain of the Adventurers inhibiting all others to buy cloths to be exported, but the merchants of their own company.

4. This privilege is divided into many petty companies for several countries where cloth may be vented inso much that to transport cloth into Muscovia none do buy cloth but one ...... Freeman.

5. Out of this privilege are also derived contracts with certain towns and companies of strangers in foreign nations to deliver the English white cloths at those towns only.

6. Thence is also derived the inhibition that some countries or places cannot buy immediately but that cloth must first be sold (for example) to the Hollanders before it can come to the subjects of the Archduchess receiving a great imposition for licence money to pass to the prejudice of the English.

7. Out of this privilege is derived a power of imposing upon every cloth sold in Blackwell Hall to be exported (since the treaty with Sir William Cocken did end) to the value of 7s. 6d. upon long cloths amounting unto (if vent were as it hath been) above 20,000li per annum.

8. Thence is also derived a power to restrain any of their own company in buying to a small number of cloths whereby the clothier being disappointed of sale is driven of necessity to undersell others for buying (not of the company) having been kept in prison till they have taken oath or entered into bonds to forbear.

9. Proof is offered in particular cases that none will buy John a Stiles cloth but he shall be driven to sell to John a Downe, his old chapman, at his price and pleasure by combination.

10. And also the cloths of such a country shall not be bought as for instance from the 21 of April until the 17 of May not one Woster cloth

hath been bought in Blackwell Hall, although confessed as seasonable as any, and the clothier, seeking to sell to the Adventurer, receiveth answer that he may do well to sell to their new company, so little compassion is shewed by them in this time of so great necessity, and so great presumption of the advantage by this privilege, having the clothiers in their mercy . . . .

12. The impositions and customs were never in any time so great nor these all at once in use and likewise in Holland and other places, whereby hath been proved that a cloth sold by the clothier at 5li price hath before it be cut in Holland for use had 4li. 13s. 4d. more laid upon it (admitting what is laid by the Hollanders for licence money 5li. 1s. 0d.).

. . . . The help and means of relief in the trade of clothing:]

1. It is humbly desired that there may be free trade of buying and selling, leaving only order for government that the credit of cloths truly made may be maintained without power in any company to be continued either of imposing or exacting any valuable sum for admission into the company, clearing the monopoly of red wood and other monopolies laying burthens upon clothing.

2. That what cloth the Merchant Adventurer will not buy off upon Thursday, it may be lawful for any person, denizen or stranger . . . on the Friday or Saturday to buy as well as he and to export without restraint whither they please.

3. That transportation of cloth may be made oftener viz. once a month, and his Majesty's shipping may (at the charge of the merchant) for their sureties waft over the merchandises as need shall require.

4. That endeavour be used that the imposition for licence in foreign countries may be moderated and that free passage may be had wheresoever best sale with least burden may be gotten, stirring up foreign nations to strive for the trade of English cloths with the best conditions a nation may gain.

5. That his Majesty will take into his princely consideration the present necessity of his clothiers and many thousands depending upon them and what the several charges are laid upon cloths all now in use, submitting to his singular and deep judgement that if all new and late charges were taken off, yet a reparation might be made of all dues to his Majesty if all the wools of England and Ireland be manufactured and so cheap afforded into other countries (with the employment of infinite people) that no other country could be able to gain by the making of cloth.

6. That no wools, wool fells, yarn or fullers earth be conveyed beyond the seas to any place out of England, Scotland, Ireland, and the Isles.

7. That foreign commodities be brought into this land either by sale of our cloth there first made or by bartering for our English cloth.
8. The reasons and proofs of benefit that will come by free trade are confirmed by the experience made about the year '87 when, for the remedying of a like inconvenience, a staple of cloths was kept at Westminster and likewise when the new company was set up, upon the project of Sir William Cockin, which presently took of cloth to the benefit of all sorts of people.

**B.M. Addenda, MS 34217, F.10**

*Acknowledgements*
Extract 21 is from a Crown-copyright record in the Leicestershire Record Office and appears by permission of The Controller of H. M. Stationery Office, as do the Transcripts of Crown-copyright Access in the Public Record Office. The British Museum, the Bodleian Library, Lambeth Palace Library and individual Record offices have kindly given their permission for the inclusion of extracts acknowledged to them. The Lichfield Diocesan Registrar kindly gave permission for the inclusion of Extract 2, the Marquess of Anglesey for Extract 18 and the Church Commissioners for Extracts 31 and 32.

# Abbreviations

| | |
|---|---|
| B.M. | British Museum |
| C.S.P.D. | Calendar of State Papers Domestic |
| L.J.R.O. | Lichfield Joint Record Office |
| L.C.R.O. | Leicester County Record Office |
| L.P.L. | Lambeth Palace Library |
| K.C.R.O. | Kent County Record Office |
| P.C.C. | Prerogative Court of Canterbury |
| N.N.R.O. | Norfolk and Norwich Record Office |
| P.R.O. | Public Record Office |
| S.C.R.O. | Staffordshire County Record Office |
| AgrHR | Agricultural History Review |
| BIHR | Bulletin of the Institute of Historical Research |
| BJES | British Journal of Educational Studies |
| EcHR | Economic History Review |
| JEH | Journal of Ecclesiastical History |
| P&P | Past and Present |
| TRHS | Transactions of the Royal Historical Society |
| UBHJ | University of Birmingham Historical Journal |

# Further Reading

ARTICLES

D. Charman 'Wealth and Trade in Leicester in the Early Sixteenth Century', *Leics. Arch. Soc.*, 1949

L. A. Clarkson 'The Organization of the English Leather Industry in the Late Sixteenth and Seventeenth Centuries', *EcHR*, 1960

D. C. Coleman 'London Scriveners and the Estate Market in the Later Seventeenth Century', *EcHR*, 1951–2

J. Cornwall 'English Country Towns in the Fifteen Twenties', *EcHR*, 1962

D. Cressey 'Occupations, Migration and Literacy in East London, 1580–1640', *Local Population Studies*, 1970

C. Cross 'The Economic Problems of the See of York: Decline and Recovery in the Sixteenth Century', *AgrHR*, Supplement, 1970

D. W. Crossley 'The Management of a Sixteenth-Century Ironworks', *EcHR*, 1966

F. R. H. Du Boulay 'Archbishop Cranmer and the Canterbury Temporalities', *EcHR*, 1952

A. Everitt 'Social Mobility in Early Modern England', *P&P*, 1966

F. J. Fisher 'The Development of the London Food Market', *EcHR*, 1937

'Some Experiments in Company Organization in the Early Seventeenth Century', *EcHR*, 1933

'Commercial Trends and Policy in Sixteenth-Century England', *EcHR*, 1940

'The Development of London as a Centre of Conspicuous Consumption in the Sixteenth and Seventeenth Centuries', *TRHS*, 1948

'London's Export Trade in the Early Seventeenth Century', *EcHR*, 1950

'Influenza and Inflation in Tudor England', *EcHR*, 1965

J. D. Gould 'The Trade Depression of the Early 1620s', *EcHR*, 1954

H. J. Habakkuk 'The Long-term Rate of Interest and the Price of Land in the Seventeenth Century', *EcHR*, 1952

'The Market for Monastic Property, 1539–1603', *EcHR*, 1957–8

F. Heal 'The Tudors and Church Lands: Economic Problems of the Bishopric of Ely during the Sixteenth Century,' *EcHR*, 1973
'The Bishops and the Act of Exchanges of 1559', *Historical Journal*, 1974
R. W. K. Hinton 'The Mercantile System in the Time of Thomas Mun', *EcHR*, 1955
W. G. Hoskins 'English Provincial Towns in the Early Sixteenth Century', *TRHS*, 1956
'The Elizabethan Merchants of Exeter', in *Elizabethan Government and Society*, S. T. Bindoff, J. Hurstfield & C. H. Williams (eds.), 1961
C. J. Kitching 'The Quest for Concealed Lands in the Reign of Elizabeth I,' *TRHS* 24, 1974
J. U. Nef 'The Progress of Technology and the Growth of Large-scale Industry in Great Britain, 1540–1640', *EcHR*, 1934
R. O'Day 'Church Records and the History of Education', *History of Education*, 1973
'Thomas Bentham. . . .' *JEH*, 1972
'Cumulative Debt: The Approach of the Bishops of Lichfield to their Economic Problems from the Reformation to the Civil War', *Midland History*, 1975
R. B. Outhwaite 'The Price of Crown Land at the Turn of the Sixteenth Century', *EcHR*, 1967
'The Trials of Foreign Borrowing: The English Crown and the Antwerp Money Market in the Mid-Sixteenth Century', *EcHR*, 1966
'Who Bought Crown Lands? The Pattern of Purchases 1589–1603', *BIHR*, 1971
J. F. Pound 'An Elizabethan Census of the Poor', *UBHJ*, 1962
E. E. Rich 'The Population of Elizabethan England', *EcHR*, 1950
K. R. M. Short 'A Theory of Common Education in Elizabethan Puritanism', *JEH*, 1972
B. Simon 'Leicestershire Schools, 1625–40', *BJES*, 1954–5
M. Spufford 'The Schooling of the Peasantry in Cambridgeshire Shire, 1575–1700', *AgrHR*, Supplement, 1970
L. Stone 'State Control in Sixteenth-Century England', EcHR, 1947
'An Elizabethan Coal Mine', *EcHR*, 1950
'The Nobility in Business', *The Entrepreneur*, 1957
'The Educational Revolution in England, 1560–1640', *P&P*, 1964
'Social Mobility in England, 1500–1700', *P&P*, 1966
'Literacy and Education in England, 1640–1900', *P&P*, 1969

**BOOKS**


P. Aries *Centuries of Childhood* (transl.), Cape 1962

M. Ashley *Financial and Commercial Policy under the Cromwellian Protectorate*, F. Cass 1962

R. Ashton *The Crown and the Money Market*, Oxford University Press 1960

P. J. Bowden *The Wool Trade in Tudor and Stuart England*, F. Cass, 2nd ed. 1971

M. Campbell *The English Yeoman under Elizabeth and the Early Stuarts*, Merlin Press 1942

C. W. Chalklin *Seventeenth-Century Kent: A Social and Economic History*, Longmans 1965

J. D. Chambers *Population, Economy and Society in Pre-Industrial England*, Oxford University Press 1972

C. M. Cipolla *Literacy and Development in the West*, Penguin 1969

P. Clark & P. Slack (eds.) *Crisis and Order in English Towns, 1500–1700*, Routledge 1972

L. A. Clarkson *The Pre-Industrial Economy in England, 1500–1750*, Batsford 1971

J. T. Cliffe *The Yorkshire Gentry*, Athlone Press 1969

P. S. Crowson *Tudor Foreign Policy*, Black 1973

R. Davis *English Overseas Trade*, Macmillan 1973

*The Rise of the Atlantic Economies*, Weidenfeld & Nicolson, 1973

F. C. Dietz *English Government Finance, 1485–1558*, F. Cass 1964

O. J. Dunlop & R. D. Denham *English Apprenticeship and Child Labour*, 1912

A. D. Dyer *The City of Worcester in the Sixteenth Century*, Leicester University Press, 1973

G. R. Elton *Reform and Renewal*, Cambridge University Press 1973

A. Everitt *Change in the Provinces: The Seventeenth Century*, Leicester University Press 1969

M. A. Finch *The Wealth of Five Northamptonshire Families, 1540–1640*, Northants. Record Society 1966

W. P. Haugaard *Elizabeth and the English Reformation*, Cambridge University Press 1968

P. Hembry *The Bishops of Bath and Wells*, Athlone Press 1967

D. G. Hey *An English Rural Community: Myddle under the Tudors and Stuarts*, Leicester University Press 1974

C. Hill *Economic Problems of the Church*, Oxford University Press 1956

*Reformation to Industrial Revolution*, Weidenfeld & Nicolson 1967

J. W. F. Hill *Tudor and Stuart Lincoln*, Cambridge University Press 1956
T. H. Hollingsworth *Historical Demography*, Hodder 1969
D. Hollis (ed.) *Calendar of the Bristol Apprentice Book*, 1532–65, 1949
G. M. D. Howat *Stuart and Cromwellian Foreign Policy*, Black 1974
M. James *Family, Lineage and Civil Society*, Oxford University Press
H. Kearney *Scholars and Gentlemen*, Faber & Faber 1970
E. Kerridge *The Agricultural Revolution*, Allen & Unwin 1967
P. Laslett *The World We Have Lost*, Methuen 1971
W. T. MacCaffrey *Exeter, 1540–1640: The Growth of an English Country Town*, Oxford University Press 1958
A. Macfarlane *The Family Life of Ralph Josselin*, Cambridge University Press 1970
R. O'Day & F. Heal *Continuity and Change: Personnel and Administration of the Church in England*, 1500–1642, Leicester University Press 1975
R. B. Outhwaite *Inflation in Tudor and Early Stuart England*, Macmillan 1969
I. Pinchbeck & M. Hewitt *Children in English Society*, vol. 1, Routledge 1969
J. F. Pound *The Norwich Census of the Poor*, 1570, Norfolk Record Society 1972
W. R. Prest *The Inns of Court*, 1590–1640, Longmans 1972
P. H. Ramsey (ed.) *The Price Revolution in Sixteenth-Century England*, Methuen 1971
O. & P. Ranum (eds.) *Popular Attitudes toward Birth Control in Pre-Industrial France and England*, Harper & Row 1973
M. M. Reese *The Puritan Impulse*, Black 1975
C. Russell (ed.) *The Origins of the English Civil War*, Macmillan 1973
J. Simon *Education and Society in Tudor England*, Cambridge University Press 1966
A. Simpson *The Wealth of the Gentry*, 1540–1660, Cambridge University Press 1961
A. G. R. Smith (ed.) *The Reign of James VI and I*, Macmillan 1973
W. B. Stephens *Seventeenth-Century Exeter*, University of Exeter 1958
L. Stone *The Crisis of the Aristocracy*, 1558–1641, Oxford University Press 1965
*Family and Fortune*, Oxford University Press 1973
B. E. Supple *Commercial Crisis and Change*, Cambridge University Press 1959

R. H. Tawney *Religion and the Rise of Capitalism*, Murray 1926, Penguin 1969

J. Thirsk (ed.) *Agrarian History of England and Wales*, IV, Cambridge University Press 1967

G. S. L. Tucker *Progress and Profits in British Economic Thought*, Cambridge University Press 1960

F. Watson *The Beginnings of the Teaching of Modern Subjects in England*, S. R. Publishers repub. 1971

A. J. Willis & A. L. Merson (eds.) *A Calendar of Southampton Apprenticeship Registers*, 1609–1740, Southampton University 1968

C. Wilson *England's Apprenticeship*, 1603–1763, Longmans 1965, 1971; *Profit and Power*, Longmans 1957

J. Youings *The Dissolution of the Monasteries*, Allen & Unwin 1972

# Glossary

APPROPRIATION a benefice made over to a monastery or corporation, which drew the great tithes, was responsible for the upkeep of the chancel and parsonage and, normally, was also charged with the provision of a vicar (substitute) to serve the cure

ENTRY FINE in the case of copyhold tenure—particularly where held for a life or a number of years—the copyholder paid an entry fine which was arbitrarily fixed upon by the lord; in almost half the copyholds by inheritance, the entry fine was fixed and certain at about twice the annual rent. Increasingly, however, the fines were certain but fixed at twice the annual *improved value* of the holding

IMPROPRIATION an ecclesiastical benefice placed in the hands of a layman, who drew the great tithes, and was responsible for the upkeep of the chancel and parsonage house, and was often the patron of the vicarage

IN COMMENDAM an ecclesiastical benefice granted to an official, for a set time and without duties, on condition that he appoint a curate out of the proceeds of the benefice

20 YEARS' PURCHASE Crown (including monastic) property was normally sold at a rate of 20 times the annual value of the property as assessed

SEDE VACANTE term signifying a vacant see

SUBSIDY a parliamentary (or, in the case of the clergy of the realm, a convocational) grant to the Crown of a levy of so much in the pound on assessed income

TITHE the tenth of the produce of land and stock allotted for church purposes; sometimes a rent-charge in commutation of this. Tithes were normally divided into the great and the small tithes—the great (Corn) tithes were normally in the possession of the lay or clerical rector, while the small tithes were owned by the vicar.

# Index